BREAD MACHINE COOKBOOK
FOR BEGINNERS

REDISCOVER THE PLEASURE OF HAVING WARM AND CRISPY LOAF EVERY DAY.
THE COMPLETE GUIDE TO PREPARING MANY SIMPLE AND TASTY RECIPES WITHOUT STRESS

PAULA ALLEN

Introduction...7

What Is A Bread Machine?...13

What Are The Most Common Ingredients...23

Tips And Tricks In Order

To Have A Better Final Product

And To Save Money And Time...31

1 - Basic White Bread ... 37

2 - Gluten Free Bread ... 38

3 - All- Purpose White Bread ... 39

4 - Anadama Bread ... 40

5 - Apricot Bread ... 41

6 - Green Cheese Braed ... 42

7 - French Cheese Bread ... 43

8 - Beer Cheese Bread ... 44

9 - Jalapeno Cheese Bread ... 45

10 - Cheddar Cheese Bread ... 46

11 - Cottage Cheese And Chive Bread ... 47

12 - Ricotta Bread ... 48

13 - Oregano Cheese Bread ... 49

14 - Spinach And Feta Bread ... 50

15 - Italian Cheese Bread ... 51

16 - Curd Bread ... 52

17 - Original Italian Herb Bread ... 53

18 - Lovely Aromatic Lavender Bread ... 54

19 - Cinnamon & Dried Bread ... 55

20 - Herbal Garlic Cream Cheese Bread ... 56

21 - Oregano Mozza-Cheese Bread ... 57

22 - Cumin Tossed Fancy Bread ... 58

23 - Potato Rosemary Loaf ... 59

24 - Delicius Honey Lavender Bread ... 60

25 - Inspiring Cinnamon Bread ... 61

26 - Lavander Buttermilk Bread ... 62

27 - Cajun Bread ... 63

28 - Turmeric Braed ... 64

29 - Rosemary Cranberry Pecan Bread ... 65

30 - Sesame French Bread ... 66

31 - Herb Bread ... 67

32 - Original Italian Herb Bread ... 68

33 - Cumin Bread ... 69

34 - Saffron Tomato Bread ... 70

35 - Peaches And Cream Bread ...71

36 - Warm Spiced Pumpkin Bread ... 72

37 - Pure Peach Bread ... 73

38 - Blueberry Honey Bread ... 74

39 - Sunflower & Flax Seed ... 75

40 - Nutritious 9-Grain Brea ... 76

41 - Oatmeal Sunflower Bread ... 77

42 - Cornmeal Whole Wheat Bread ... 78

43 - Delicious Cranberry Bread ... 79

44 - Coffee Raisin Bread ... 80

45 - Healthy Multigrain Bread ... 81

46 - Italian Pine Nut Bread ... 82

47 - Whole Wheat Raisin Bread ... 83

48 - Healthy Spelt Bread ... 84

49 - Awesome Rosemary Bread ... 85

50 - Herbed Baguette ... 86

51 - Pumpernickel Bread ... 87

52 - Honey Sourdough Bread ... 88

53 - Multigrain Sourdough Bread ... 89

54 - Olive And Garlic Sourdough Bread ... 90

55 - Herbed Baguette ... 91

56 - Sauerkraut Rye Bread ... 92

57 - French Bread Sourdough Bread ... 93

58 - Sourdough Starter Bread ... 94

59 - Mom's White Bread ... 95

60 - Vegan White Bread ... 96

61 - Rice Flour Rice Bread ... 97

62 - Italian White Bread ... 98

63 - Anadama White Bread ... 99

64 - Soft White Bread ... 100

65 - English Muffin Bread ... 101

66 - Cranberry Orange Breakfast Bread ... 102

67 - Buttermilk Honey Bread ... 103

68 - Whole Wheat Breakfast Bread ... 104

69 - Cinnamon-Raisin Bread ... 105

70 - Butter Bread Rolls ... 106

71 - Cranberry & Golden Raisin Bread ... 107

72 - Brown & White Sugar Bread ... 108

73 - Molasses Bread ... 109

74 - Honey Bread ... 110

75 - Maple Syrup Bread ... 111

76 - Raisin Bread ... 112

77 - Currant Bread ... 113

78 - Pineapple Juice Bread ... 114

79 - Pumpkin Bread ... 115

80 - Pumpkin Cranberry Bread ... 116

81 - Cranberry Bread ... 117

82 - Cranberry Orange Bread ... 118

83 - Orange Bread ... 119

84 - Banana Chocolate Chip Bread ... 120

85 - Sweet Potato Bread ... 121

86 - Gingerbread ... 122

87 - Chocolate Chip Bread ... 123

88 - Seed And Nut Bread ... 124

89 - Pizza Basis ... 125

90 - Italian Pie Calzone ... 126

91 - French Baguettes ... 127

92 - Unleavened Cornbread ... 128

93 - Vegan Corn Bread ... 129

94 - Milk And Honey Bread ... 130

95 - Banana Bread ... 131

96 - Salt Crusted Bread ... 132

97 - Extra Buttery White Bread ... 133

Conclusion... 134

Conversion Tables ... 138

6

INTRODUCTION

Even if you are not good at using modern appliances, leave your worries behind. Bread machines have simple and user-friendly controls and using them is fun and easy!

Bread is an everyday staple. A food item we regularly purchase, buying store-bought bread is undoubtedly convenient. However, store-bought bread is packed with chemical additives, extra sugars, and salts to ensure longer shelf life.

To gauge how baking your own bread is worth it, do yourself a favor; look at the label on the back of store-bought bread and compare it to the list of ingredients needed to make your own. You will notice the stark contrast of ingredients. Store-bought includes emulsifiers and agents, but a basic bread recipe is made up of very few affordable ingredients, none of which include words that I even struggle pronouncing. And when you look at the bigger picture, you'll see you are better off baking your own bread, especially with quite a convenient and useful tool, such as a bread machine.

There are many pros to making bread at home, including the fact that it is far tastier than your standard, mass-produced bread. You can alter ingredients, meaning you have more control over the sugar, fiber, Protein: and salt content. You can also get inventive by adding in nuts and dried fruits. Buying your own ingredients means you can manage all of what goes in the machine and provides you the opportunity of seeking the freshest ingredients.

Advantages of Bread Machines

A bread machine does it all instead of you

This means you will be able to avoid kitchen mess, as the bread machine does everything from mixing to kneading to baking.

Yes, it sounds like magic, but it is for real. Just imagine warm bread and a clean kitchen. Dreams can come true!

Bread machines keep your health under control

By this, we mean that you can choose the ingredients you want and create a bread that is carb-free and free of any additives that might cause harm to your body. This feature is very appreciated by those who follow the keto diet. You can make your own bread that is much better than the store-bought version, at a low cost, and you know it was created in a clean environment where cross-contamination is not possible.

A bread machine allows you to have fresh, warm bread every day

This is perhaps the most obvious benefit of a bread-making machine. Most bread machines have a time function you can set to have your bread ready at a certain time. This is very useful, as it allows you to prepare the ingredients and then continue with your daily chores, while the bread machine does everything else for you. Just imagine, you are coming home after an exhausting day of work, and warm, delicious bread is waiting for you!

Bread machines save money

Yes, bread machines may be expensive initially, but buying bread every day, or even just every week, is more costly.

Not to mention all of that thrown away bread, the stale bread that no one wants to eat anymore. With each slice, you are throwing away your money. The bread machine maker allows you to make smaller or larger loaves and ones that fit your family's dietary and consumption habits. Besides, making bread from scratch is always cheaper than buying it at the store.

Bread machines produce better quality bread

Fresh bread is fresh bread, and no store-bought version can compete with that. In addition, what about that chewy, rubber-like bread you sometimes get? Something like that will never happen to you with a bread-making machine. The homemade bread is made with natural ingredients and does not have any artificial additives. The additives that are used in store-bought bread can keep it fresher for a longer time, but they affect the texture. It is always better to make bread fresh and additive-free than to eat "fake-fresh" bread for days.

Bread machines are easy to use

The bread machine looks like a simple appliance, and believe us, it is. If you are not good with the baking process and somehow you always end up with over- or under-cooked foods, you can skip this worry, as the bread-making machine bakes everything to perfection.

Bread making machines make more than bread

The bread machine can be used for many other purposes besides making bread. You can use it to make a baguette, sweet breads, and even dough. The possibilities are endless.

These are just some of the advantages of a bread machine. We are sure you will soon discover others and learn to appreciate the many uses of a bread machine. And while that happens, we suggest you enjoy our recipe collection from this book.

I'm a wonderful bread machine!

WHAT IS A BREAD MACHINE?

A bread machine is a kitchen appliance for heating bread. The gadget is a shovel or bread tin, made in the spatulas, which is located in the center of a small multifunctional original mesh.

How Is Bread Machine Made?

This machine is essentially a conservative electric appliance that holds a solitary, huge bread tin inside. The tin itself is somewhat extraordinary – it has a hub at the base that is associated with an electric engine underneath.

A little metal oar is appended to the pivot at the base of the tin. The oar is answerable for manipulating the mixture. A waterproof seal secures the hub itself. We should investigate every one of the bread machine parts in detail:

- The top over the bread producer comes either with the survey window or without it.

- The control board is likewise situated on the highest point of the bread machine with the end goal of comfort.

.

- **I**n the focal point of the top, there is a steam vent that depletes the steam during the heating procedure. A portion of the bread creators likewise have an air vent on the gadget for air to come inside the tin for the mixture to rise .

Benefits of a Bread Machine

While utilizing a bread machine for some may seem like a pointless advance, others don't envision the existence without newly home-heated bread. In any case, how about we go to the realities – underneath, we indicated the advantages of owning a bread machine.

As a matter of first importance, you can appreciate the crisply prepared handcrafted bread. Most bread creators additionally include a clockwork, which permits you to set the preparing cycle at a specific time. This capacity is extremely valuable when you need to have sweltering bread toward the beginning of the day for breakfast.

You can control what you eat. By preparing bread at home, you can really control what parts are coming into your portion. This choice is extremely valuable for individuals with sensitivities or for those, who attempt to control the admission of a fixings' portion.

It is simple. A few people believe that preparing bread at home is chaotic, and by and large, it is a hard procedure. In any case, preparing bread with a bread machine is a breeze.

You simply pick the ideal choice and unwind - all the blending, rising, and heating process is going on within the bread producer, which additionally makes it a zero chaos process! It sets aside your huge amounts of cash in the long haul. If you imagine that purchasing bread at a store is modest, you may be mixed up. In turns out that in the long haul, preparing bread at home will set aside your cash, particularly in the event that you have some dietary limitations.

Incredible taste and quality, you have to acknowledge it – nothing beats the quality and taste of a crisp heap of bread. Since you are the person who is making bread, you can ensure that you utilize just the fixings that are new and of a high caliber. Homemade bread consistently beats locally acquired bread as far as taste and quality.

How Does Bread Machine Work?

To begin with, you put the plying paddle i nside the tin. At the point when the tin is out of the machine, you can gauge the fixings and burden them into the tin.

A while later, you simply need to put the skillet inside the stove (machine), pick the program you wish by means of the electronic board, and close the top. Here the bread producer enchantment dominates!

One of the main things the bread machine will do is wor king the batter – you will hear the sounds.

On the off chance that your bread creator accompanies the preview window, you can watch the entire procedure of preparing, which is very interesting.

After the massaging stage, everything will go calm for quite a while – the rising stage comes.

The machine allows the mixture to dough and rise. At that point, there will be another round of manipulating and a period of demonstrating.

Although the typical bread making process is programmed, most machines accompany formula books that give you various intriguing propelled bread plans.

The best thing about using a bread-making machine is it gets the hard cycle of bread making easy. You can use the bread-making machine in complete cycle, especially for loaf bread, or you can just do the dough cycle if you are baking bread that needs to bake in an oven. To use the bread-making machine, here are some steps to guide you.

Familiarize yourself with the parts and buttons of your bread-making machine

Your bread-making machine has three essential parts, and without it, you will not be able to cook your bread. The first part is the machine itself, the second is the bread bucket, and the third is the kneading blade. The bread bucket and kneading blade are removable and replaceable. You can check with the manufacturer for parts to replace it if it's missing.

Learn how to operate your bread-making machine. Removing and placing the bread bucket back in is important. Practice snapping the bread bucket on and off the machine until you are comfortable doing it. This is important because you don't want the bucket moving once the ingredients are in place.

Know your bread bucket capacity

This is an important step before you start using the machine. If you load an incorrect measurement, you are going to have a big mess on your hand. To check your bread bucket capacity:

·Use a liquid measuring cup and fill it with water.

·Pour the water on the bread bucket until it's full. Count how many cups of water you poured on the bread bucket.

·The number of cups of water will determine the size of your loaf bread:

·Less than 10 cups =1-pound loaf

·10 cups =1 to 1 ½ pounds loaf

·12 cups=1 or 1 ½ to 2 pounds loaf

·14 cups or more=1 or ½ to 2 or 2 ½ pounds loaf

Learn the basic buttons and settings of your bread-making machine

The buttons indicate the cycle in which your machine will mix, knead, and bake the bread. Familiarize yourself with the parts and buttons of your bread-making machine.

Your bread-making machine has three essential parts. The first part is the machine itself, the second is the bread bucket, and the third is the kneading blade.

The bread bucket and kneading blade are removable and replaceable. You can check with the manufacturer for parts to replace it if it's missing

- Basic buttons include **START/STOP**, **CRUST COLOR**, **TIMER/ARROW**, **SELECT (BASIC, SWEET, WHOLE WHEAT, FRENCH, GLUTEN FREE, QUICK/RAPID, QUICK BREAD, JAM, DOUGH.)**

The **SELECT** button allows you to choose the cycle you want in which you want to cook your loaf. It also includes DOUGH cycle for oven-cooked breads.

Using the Delay button

When you select a cycle, the machine sets a preset timer to bake the bread. For example, if you select BASIC, time will be set by 3 hours. However, you want your bread cooked at a specific time, say, you want it in the afternoon, but it's only 7:00 in the morning. Your bread cooks for 3 hours, which means it will be done by 10:00 am, but you want it done by 12.

You can use the up and down arrow key to set the delay timer. Between 7 am and 12 noon, there is a difference of 5 hours, so you want your timer to be set at 5. Press the arrow keys up to add 2 hours in your timer so that your bread will cook in 5 hours instead of 3 hours. Delay button does not work if you are using the DOUGH cycle.

Order of adding the ingredients

This only matters if you are using the delay timer. It is important to ensure that your yeast will not touch any liquid so as not to activate it early.

Early activation of the yeast could make your bread rise too much. If you plan to start the cycle immediately, you can add the ingredients in any order. However, adding the ingredients in order will discipline you to do it every time and make you less likely to forget it when necessary. To add the ingredients, do it in the following order:

- First, place all the liquid ingredients in the bread bucket.
- Add the sugar and the salt.
- Add the flour to cover and seal in the liquid ingredients.
- Add all the other remaining dry ingredients.
- Lastly, add the yeast. The yeast should not touch any liquid until the cooking cycle starts. When adding the yeast, make a small well using your finger to place the yeast to ensure proper timing of yeast activation.

Using the Dough Cycle

You cannot cook all breads using the bread-making machine, but you can use the machine to make the bread-making process easier.

All bread goes under the dough cycle. If your bread needs to be oven-cooked, you can still use the bread-making machine by selecting the DOUGH cycle to mix and knead your flour into a dough.

To start the Dough cycle:

- Add all your bread recipe ingredients in your bread bucket.
- Select the DOUGH cycle. This usually takes between 40 to 90 minutes.
- Press the START button.
- After the cycle is complete, let your dough rest in the bread-making machine for 5 to 40 minutes.
- Take out the dough and start cutting into your desire shape.
-

Some machines have various Dough cycle, which you can use for muffin recipes. However, if all you have is basic dough setting, you can use it for muffin recipe, but you need to stop the machine before the rising cycle begins.

How to use a bread machine

Even if you're not good at using modern appliances, put your worries behind you, because bread machines have simple, easy-to-use controls.

They are fun and easy to use! Besides making fresh bread, they can also make and knead any type of dough, bake dough out of the box, and even make dough jam. When you get to know this handy device, it will truly become an essential and exceptional aid in your kitchen. It's so simple!

1. -Insert the baking sheet into the machine.
2. -Attach the dough blades.
3. -Add ingredients as shown in your machine manual.
4. -Close the lid.
5. -Turn on the machine.
6. -Select the required function.

What Else Can It Do?

Different bread machines may differ in their design, capacity, number of accessories, and programs available. When choosing your bread machine, think of your own preferences and needs: What will you do with the machine? Do you need any particular programs and additional modes, or is the basic functionality enough?

Bread machines can knead the dough, let it rest, bake a crunchy baguette, make sweet cupcakes or unleavened bread, and much more.

WHAT ARE THE MOST COMMON INGREDIENTS

Water/Milk

All of the other basic bread ingredients, including flour, salt, and yeast, need a liquid medium to do their respective tasks. Water is the most common liquid ingredient; milk, buttermilk, cream, and juice are some common substitutes.

The liquid is usually the first ingredient to be added to the bread pan. This is very important as it maintains the ideal texture of your bread. The liquid should not be cold; ensure that it is lukewarm (between 80 and 90°F) whenever possible.

Butter/Oil

Butter, oil, or fat is usually added after the liquid. This is what gives bread crust its attractive brown color and crispy texture. Do not use cold butter that has just been taken out of the refrigerator. You can either microwave it for a few seconds or keep it at room temperature until it gets soft.

Sugar/honey (if using)

Sweet ingredients such as honey, corn syrup, maple syrup, and sugar are usually added after the butter as they mix easily with water and butter. However, the sweetener can be added before the butter as well. Sugar, honey, etc. serve as a feeding medium for yeast, so fermentation is stronger with the addition of sweet ingredients.

Eggs (if using)

Eggs need to be at room temperature before they are added to the bread pan. If the eggs are taken from the refrigerator, keep them outside at room temperature until they are no longer cold. They keep the crust tender and add protein and flavor to the bread.

Salt

Use table salt or non-iodized salt for better results. Salt that is high in iodine can hamper the activity of the yeast and create problems with fermentation. Furthermore, salt itself is a yeast inhibitor and should not be touching yeast directly; that is why salt and yeast are never added together or one after another.

Spices (if using)

Spices such as cinnamon, nutmeg, and ginger are often used to add flavor to the bread. They may be added before or after the flour.

Flour

Flour is the primary ingredient for any bread recipe. It contains gluten (except for the gluten-free flours) and protein, and when the yeast produces alcohol and carbon dioxide, the gluten and protein trap the alcohol and carbon dioxide to initiate the bread-making process.

There are many different types of flours used for preparing different types of bread. Bread machine flour or white bread flour is the most common type as it is suitable for most bread recipes. It's so versatile because it contains an ideal proportion of protein for bread baking.

Usually, flour is stored at room temperature, but if you keep your flour in your fridge, allow it to warm up before using it.

Seeds (if using)

If a recipe calls for adding seeds such as sunflower seeds or caraway seeds, these should be added after the flour. However, when two different flours are being used, it is best to add the seeds in between the flours for a better mix.

Spices (if using)

Spices such as cinnamon, nutmeg, and ginger are often used to add flavor to the bread. They may be added before or after the flour.

Yeast

Yeast is the ingredient responsible for initiating the vital bread-making process of fermentation. Yeast needs the right amount of heat, moisture and liquid to grow and multiply. When yeast multiplies, it releases alcohol and carbon dioxide.

You can use active dry yeast or bread machine yeast (both will be available in local grocery stores). Cool, dry places are ideal to store yeast packs.

Yeast is added to the bread pan last, after the flour and other dry ingredients. (For certain types of bread, like fruit and nut bread, yeast is technically not the last ingredient, as the fruits or nuts are added later by the machine. However, yeast is the last ingredient to be added before starting the bread machine.)

Some Suggestions About Ingredients

Let's start with the flour! It is an entire world but, to simplify things a little, we will say that it is nothing more than the result of the grinding of a cereal, seed, or tuber. The most common flours for baking are wheat flour (there are many varieties of this cereal); oats; corn; rye; barley and even nuts like chestnut. It is fundamental to know the behavior of this basic ingredient since the result of the dough will be very different according to the grinding and the cereal used. As the flour that is used more frequently is that of wheat, we will focus on it (although without stopping - for now - in its varieties).

In general terms, we could say that wheat flour is composed of starch and other elements (in variable proportions) such as minerals, vitamins, proteins, and ashes. The sifting of the milling influences these factors. The whole grain, keeping the bran, make up the whole flours; if they are deprived of it, we will obtain white flours. There are flours of soft wheat and durum wheat, the difference of these lying in the amount of protein that each contains and, therefore, the result of the bread will be different. The proteins (gliadin and glutenin) that are in the flour are the main things responsible for the formation and elasticity of the dough that, together with the fermentation, makes the bread have volume and consistency.

As the flour is hydrated, the proteins bind, transforming into gluten. When we manipulate a bread dough, and they are oxygenated, the dough becomes elastic and workable. If the mass is well hydrated and kneaded, a protein mesh (glutinous network) is created that covers it. The more protein the flour has, the more water it will need, so you must be careful not to overdo it.

Yeast is the second great protagonist of bread. Typically, a fungus is used (suitable for ingestion), which can be found in two versions: dry (lyophilized) or fresh. Keep in mind that this latest version is a living organism, so it must be appropriately conserved, as it loses strength over time. If dry is used, the proportion of yeast is 1/3 of the amount indicated in the recipe for fresh. For example, if it calls for 10 gr. of fresh yeast, you should use 3 gr. of dry yeast.

Another way to produce bread is the use of natural sourdough, the oldest way to make the bread ferment (through bacteria that are present in the environment). When the bread is made with sourdough, it usually has a slightly acidic taste, lasts longer, has an intense smell, and, due to bacterial fermentation, facilitates digestion. The process of making the sourdough is simple, but it takes time (it usually takes about 5 days). Here you have a good recipe.

Water and salt have no major complications and secrets. It must be made clear that it is not necessary to use mineral water; tap water works perfectly even if some prefer to filter it. In fact, in the best professional bakeries, no water other than tap water is used. Salt brings flavor, and you can use several types of salts (marine, with herbs, etc.). In fact, the bread doesn't have to have salt; many loaves are traditionally bland, and others are brushed with a saline solution when leaving the oven (especially the loaves with little crumbs).

Flour, yeast, water, and salt are all the essential ingredients you need to make a good bread dough. Before carrying it to the oven comes the work of fermentation, kneading, etc. But as a useful note (and to encourage you to make bread), we must remember that not all the loaves are baked, nor do they need many hours of fermentation and kneading.

There is the bread that can be made in a pan, griddle, casserole, or steamed, and are an excellent option for when you do not want to heat the oven. You can also make many other pieces of bread in skillets, such as pita bread, Moroccan bread, bread from North Africa, and a variety of flatbreads. Making bread in a pan is one of the eldest ways of cooking it. If you decide to make bread in the pan, you must choose a good one that keeps the heat well and can cook evenly.

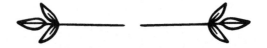

TIPS AND TRICKS IN ORDER TO HAVE A BETTER FINAL PRODUCT AND TO SAVE MONEY AND TIME

When you are using a bread machine for the first time, it's common to have some concerns. However, they are quite easy to fix. The following are some useful tips and quick-and-easy fixes for the most common problems encountered while baking bread in a bread machine.

Dough Check

You can check the progress of the dough while the bread machine is mixing the ingredients. Take a quick check after 5 minutes of kneading. An ideal dough with the right amount of dry and wet ingredients makes one smooth ball and feels slightly tacky. You can open the lid to evaluate the dough. Do not worry about interfering with the kneading process by opening the lid; the bread structure won't be affected even if you poke it to get a feel for the dough.

If the dough feels too wet/moist or does not form into a ball shape, you can add 1 tablespoon of flour at a time and check again after a few minutes. If you feel that the dough is too dry, or it has formed two or three small balls, you can add 1 teaspoon of water at a time and check again after a few minutes.

Fruit/Nut Bread

When making fruit or nut bread, it is very important to add fruits or nuts at the right time. Not all bread machines come with a nut/fruit dispenser or hopper. If yours doesn't have one, don't worry; the machine will signal you with a beep series when it's time to add the fruits or nuts.

Citrus Ingredients

Citrus ingredients such as lemon zest, orange zest, orange juice, lemon juice, and pineapple juice can create issues with yeast fermentation if added in excess. Do not add more than the quantity specified in a recipe. The same goes for alcohol and cinnamon.

Salt Adjustment

When making small loaves (around 1 pound), sometimes the loaf rises more or less than expected. In many such instances, the issue is with the quantity of salt added. To avoid problems, try using less salt or cutting back on the quantity specified in the recipe. Using sea salt or coarse salt can also help prevent problems with small loaves.

Bread Collapse

The amount of yeast is very important for proper rising. The most common reason for bread collapse during the baking process is adding too much or too little yeast. Do not add more yeast than specified in the recipe. Also, check the expiration date on the yeast pack; freshly packed yeast provides the best results. Other reasons for bread collapse are using cold water and adding excess salt.

Failure to Rise

Many factors can contribute to the failure of dough to rise completely. Insufficient gluten content, miscalculated ingredients, excess salt, excess sugar, and using cold ingredients are the most common reasons. Always warm any chilled ingredients or place them at room temperature for a while before adding them to the bread pan. However, if you are warming any ingredients in your oven, make sure not to overheat them.

They need to be lukewarm, at between 80 and 90°F, and not too hot. Also make sure that the yeast does not come in direct contact with the salt, as this creates problems with rising (that is why yeast is added last).

Texture Troubles

- If your bread has a coarse texture, try adding more salt and reducing the amount of liquid.

- If your bread looks small and feels dense, try using flour with higher protein content. Bread flour has a sufficient amount of protein, but slightly denser loaves are common when you use heavier flours such as rye flour and whole wheat flour. Use additional ingredients such as fruits, nuts, and vegetables in their specified quantities. Adding too much of such ingredients will make your loaf too heavy, small, and dense.

- Moist or gummy loaves are less common, but it can happen if you have added too much liquid or used too much sugar. Too much liquid can also result in a doughy center.

- If your bread has an unbrowned top, try adding more sugar. This can also happen if your bread machine has a glass top.

- ·If your loaf has a mushroom top, it is probably due to too much yeast or water. Try reducing the amount of water and/or yeast.

·Sometimes a baked loaf has some flour on one side. When you bake the next time, try to remove any visible flour during the kneading cycle with a rubber spatula.

- If your loaf has an overly dark crust, try using the Medium crust setting next time. This also happens if you've added too much sugar and when you fail to take out the bread pan after the end of the baking process. It is always advisable to remove the bread pan right after the process is complete.
- If your loaf has a sunken top, it is probably because of using too much liquid or overly hot ingredients. This is also common during humid or warm weather.

Chilled Ingredients

If you are using any other ingredient that is kept chilled, such as cheese, milk, buttermilk or cream, keep it outside at room temperature until it is no longer cold, or microwave it for a few seconds to warm it up.

Excess Rise

Many times, a loaf rises more than expected; the most common reasons are too much yeast, too little salt, and using cold water. But also make sure that the capacity of your bread pan is sufficient for the size of loaf you have selected; trying to make a large loaf in a small bread pan will obviously lead to such trouble.

Paddles

After the bread machine completes its baking process the paddles may remain inside the bread loaf. Allow the freshly made bread to cool down and then place it on a cutting board and gently take out the paddles. Spraying the paddles with a cooking spray before you add the ingredients to the bread pan will make it easier to clean them after the bread is baked.

Cleaning

After you take the baked loaf from the bread pan, do not immerse the pan in water. Rather, fill it with warm soapy water.

worth it for a lot of people, though.

1 - Basic White Bread

Servings 1 loaf

Difficulty ● ○ ○

Preparation Time 10 m

Cooking Time 1 h

Ingredients

- ½ to 5/8 cup Water
- 5/8 cup Milk
- 1 ½ tablespoon butter
- 3 tablespoon Sugar
- 1 ½ teaspoon Salt
- 3 cups Bread Flour
- 1 ½ teaspoon Active dry Yeast

Directions

Put all ingredients in the bread pan, using minimal measure of liquid listed in the recipe.

Select medium Crust setting and press Start. Observe the dough as it kneads.

Following 5 to 10 minutes, in the event that it seems dry and firm, or if your machine seems as though it's straining to knead, add more liquid 1 tablespoon at a time until dough forms well.

Once the baking cycle ends, remove bread from pan, and allow to cool before slicing.

Calories: 64 Cal
Fat: 1 g
Protein: 2 g
Carb: 12 g

2- Gluten Free Bread

Servings   1 loaf

Difficulty   ● ○ ○

Preparation Time   20 m

Cooking Time 4 h 30 m

Ingredients

- 2 cups rice flour Potato starch
- 1/2 cup Tapioca flour
- 1/2 cup Xanthan gum
- 2 1/2 teaspoons 2/3 cup powdered milk or 1/2 non diary substitute
- 1 1/2 teaspoons Salt
- 1 1/2 teaspoons egg substitute (optional)
- 3 tablespoons Sugar
- 1 2/3 cups lukewarm water
- 1 1/2 tablespoons Dry yeast, granules
- tablespoons Butter, melted or margarine
- 1 teaspoon Vinegar
- 3 eggs, room temperature

Directions

Add yeast to the bread pan

Add all the flours, xanthan/ gum, milk powder, salt, and sugar

Beat the eggs, and mix with water, butter, and vinegar

Choose white bread setting at medium or use 3-4 hour setting

Calories: 126 Cal
Fat: 2 g
Protein: 3 g
Carb: 29 g

3 - All-Purpose White Bread

Servings 1 loaf

Difficulty ● ○ ○

Preparation Time 20 m

Cooking Time 2 h 10 m

Ingredients

- ¾ cup water at 80 degrees F
- 1 tablespoon melted butter, cooled
- 1 tablespoon sugar
- ¾ teaspoon salt
- 2 tablespoons skim milk powder
- 2 cups white bread flour
- ¾ teaspoon instant yeast

Directions

Add all of the ingredients to your bread machine, carefully following the instructions of the manufacturer.

Set the program of your bread machine to Basic/White Bread and set crust type to Medium.

Press START.

Wait until the cycle completes.

Once the loaf is ready, take the bucket out and let the loaf cool for 5 minutes. Gently shake the bucket to remove the loaf.

Put to a cooling rack, slice, and serve.

Calories: 140 Cal
Fat: 2 g
Protein: 4 g
Carb: 27 g

4 - Anadama Bread

Servings 1 loaf

Difficulty ● ○ ○

Preparation Time 30 m

Cooking Time 3 h

Ingredients

- 1/2 cup sunflower seeds
- 2 teaspoon bread machine yeast
- 1/2 cups bread flour
- 3/4 cup yellow cornmeal
- 2 tablespoon unsalted butter, cubed
- 1 1/2 teaspoon salt
- 1/4 cup dry skim milk powder
- 1/4 cup molasses
- 1 1/2 cups water, with a temperature of 80 to 90 degrees F

Directions

Put all the ingredients in the pan, except the sunflower seeds, in this order: water, molasses, milk, salt, butter, cornmeal, flour, and yeast.

Place the pan in the machine and close the lid.

Put the sunflower seeds in the fruit and nut dispenser.

Turn the machine on and choose the basic setting and your desired color of the crust. Press starts.

Calories: 130
Fat: 2 g
Protein: 3 g
Carb: 25 g

5 - Apricot Oat

Servings 1 loaf

Difficulty ● ○ ○

Preparation Time 25 m

Cooking Time 1 h 25 m

Ingredients

- 1/4 cups bread flour
- 2/3 cup rolled oats
- 1 tablespoon white sugar
- 2 teaspoons active dry yeast
- 1 1/2 teaspoons salt
- 1 teaspoon ground cinnamon
- 2 tablespoons butter, cut up
- 1 2/3 cups orange juice
- 1/2 cup diced dried apricots
- 2 tablespoons honey, warmed

Directions

Into the pan of bread machine, put the bread ingredients in the order suggested by manufacturer.

Then pout in dried apricots before the knead cycle completes.

Immediately remove bread from machine when it's done and then glaze with warmed honey.
Let to cool completely prior to serving.

Calories: 80
Fat: 2.3 g
Protein: 1.3 g
Carb: 14.4 g

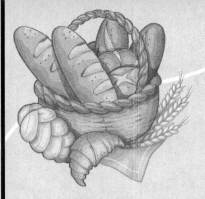

6 - Green Cheese Bread

Servings 8

Difficulty ● ● ○

Preparation Time 15 m

Cooking Time 3 h

Ingredients

- ¾ cup lukewarm water
- 1 Tablespoon sugar
- 1 teaspoon kosher salt
- Tablespoon green cheese
- 1 cup wheat bread machine flour
- 9/10 cup whole-grain flour, finely ground
- 1 teaspoon bread machine yeast
- 1 teaspoon ground paprika

Directions

Place all the dry and liquid ingredients, except paprika, in the pan and follow the instructions for your bread machine.

Pay particular attention to measuring the ingredients. Use a measuring cup, measuring spoon, and kitchen scales to do so.

Dissolve yeast in warm milk in a saucepan and add in the last turn.

Add paprika after the beep or place it in the dispenser of the bread machine.

Set the baking program to BASIC and the crust type to DARK.

If the dough is too dense or too wet, adjust the amount of flour and liquid in the recipe.

When the program has ended, take the pan out of the bread machine and let cool for 5 minutes.

Shake the loaf out of the pan. If necessary, use a spatula.

Wrap the bread with a kitchen towel and set it aside for an hour. Otherwise, you can cool it on a wire rack.

Calories: 118
Fat: 1 g
Protein: 4.1 g
Carb: 23.6 g

7 - French Cheese Bread

Servings 14 slices

Difficulty ● ● ○

Preparation Time 5 m

Cooking Time 3 h

Ingredients

- 1 teaspoon sugar
- 2¼ teaspoon yeast
- 1¼ cup water
- 3 cups bread flour
- 2 Tablespoon parmesan cheese
- 1 teaspoon garlic powder
- 1½ teaspoon salt

Directions

Add each ingredient to the bread machine in the order and at the temperature recommended by your bread machine manufacturer

Close the lid, select the basic bread, medium crust setting on your bread machine, and press START

When the bread machine has finished baking, remove the bread and put it on a cooling rack

Calories: 170
Fat: 6 g
Protein: 8 g
Carb: 21.6 g

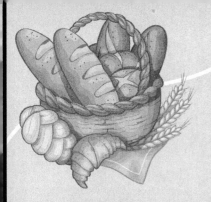

8 - Beer Cheese Bread

Servings 14 slices

Difficulty ● ● ●

Preparation Time 10 m

Cooking Time 2 h 10 m

Ingredients

- 1 package active dry yeast
- 3 cups bread flour
- 1 Tablespoon sugar
- 1½ teaspoon salt
- 1 Tablespoon room temperature butter
- 1¼ cup room temperature beer
- ½ cup shredded or diced American cheese
- ½ cup shredded or diced Monterey jack cheese

Directions

Heat the beer and American cheese in the microwave together until just warm.

Add each ingredient to the bread machine in the order and at the temperature recommended by your bread machine manufacturer.

Close the lid, select the basic bread, medium crust setting on your bread machine and press START.

When the bread machine has finished baking, remove the bread and put it on a cooling rack.

Calories: 144
Fat: 5 g
Protein: 5 g
Carb: 21 g

9 - Jalapeno Cheese Bread

Servings 14 slices

Difficulty

Preparation Time 3 m

Cooking Time 3 h

Ingredients

- 3 cups bread flour
- 1½ teaspoon active dry yeast
- 1 cup water
- 2 Tablespoon sugar
- 1 teaspoon salt
- ½ cup shredded cheddar cheese
- ¼ cup diced jalapeno peppers

Directions

Add each ingredient to the bread machine in the order and at the temperature recommended by your bread machine manufacturer.

Close the lid, select the basic bread, medium crust setting on your bread machine, and press START.

When the bread machine has finished baking, remove the bread and put it on a cooling rack.

Calories: 144
Fat: 5 g
Protein: 5 g
Carb: 21 g

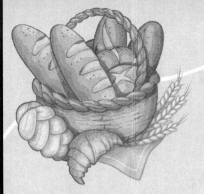

10 - Cheddar Cheese Bread

Servings 14 slices

Difficulty ● ● ○

Preparation Time 5 m

Cooking Time 3 h 10 m

Ingredients

- 1 cup lukewarm milk
- 3 cups all-purpose flour
- 1¼ teaspoon salt
- 1 teaspoon tabasco sauce, optional
- ¼ cup Vermont cheese powder
- 1 Tablespoon sugar
- 1 cup grated cheddar cheese, firmly packed
- 1 1/2 teaspoon instant yeast

Directions

Add each ingredient to the bread machine in the order and at the temperature recommended by your bread machine manufacturer.

Close the lid, select the basic bread, medium crust setting on your bread machine, and press START.

When the bread machine has finished baking, remove the bread and put it on a cooling rack.

Calories: 165
Fat: 4 g
Protein: 7 g
Carb: 25 g

11 - Cottage Cheese and Chive Bread

Servings 14 slices

Difficulty ● ● ○

Preparation Time 10 m

Cooking Time 3 h

Ingredients

- 3/8 cup water
- 1 cup cottage cheese
- 1 large egg
- 2 Tablespoon butter
- 1½ teaspoon salt
- 3¾ cups white bread flour
- 3 Tablespoon dried chives
- 2½ Tablespoon granulated sugar
- 2¼ teaspoon active dry yeast

Directions

Add each ingredient to the bread machine in the order and at the temperature recommended by your bread machine manufacturer.

Close the lid, select the basic bread, medium crust setting on your bread machine, and press START.

When the bread machine has finished baking, remove the bread and put it on a cooling rack.

Calories: 169
Fat: 4 g
Protein: 7 g
Carb: 33 g

12 - Ricotta Bread

Servings 14 slices

Difficulty

Preparation Time 5 m

Cooking Time 3 h 15 m

Ingredients

- 3 Tablespoon skim milk
- 2/3 cup ricotta cheese
- 4 teaspoon unsalted butter, softened to room temperature
- 1 large egg
- 2 Tablespoon granulated sugar
- ½ teaspoon salt
- 1½ cups bread flour, + more flour, as needed
- 1 teaspoon active dry yeast

Directions

Add each ingredient to the bread machine in the order and at the temperature recommended by your bread machine manufacturer.

Close the lid, select the basic bread, medium crust setting on your bread machine, and press START.

When the bread machine has finished baking, remove the bread and put it on a cooling rack.

Calories: 174
Fat: 12 g
Protein: 11 g
Carb: 30 g

13 - Oregano Cheese Bread

Servings   14 slices

Difficulty

Preparation Time 10m

Cooking Time 2 h 5 m

Ingredients

- 3 cups bread flour
- 1 cup water
- ½ cup freshly grated parmesan cheese
- 3 Tablespoon sugar
- 1 Tablespoon dried leaf oregano
- 1½ Tablespoon olive oil
- 1 teaspoon salt
- 2 teaspoon active dry yeast

Directions

Add each ingredient to the bread machine in the order and at the temperature recommended by your bread machine manufacturer.

Close the lid, select the basic bread, medium crust setting on your bread machine, and press START.

When the bread machine has finished baking, remove the bread and put it on a cooling rack.

Calories: 146
Fat: 5 g
Protein: 3 g
Carb: 22 g

14 - Spinach and Feta Brea

Servings 14 slices

Difficulty ● ● ○

Preparation Time 10m

Cooking Time 4 h 5 m

Ingredients

- 1 cup water
- 2 teaspoon butter
- 3 cups flour
- 1 teaspoon sugar
- 2 teaspoon instant minced onion
- 1 teaspoon salt
- 1¼ teaspoon instant yeast
- 1 cup crumbled feta
- 1 cup chopped fresh spinach leaves

Directions

Add each ingredient except the cheese and spinach to the bread machine in the order and at the temperature recommended by your bread machine manufacturer.

Close the lid, select the basic bread, medium crust setting on your bread machine, and press START.

When only 10 minutes are left in the last kneading cycle add the spinach and cheese.

When the bread machine has finished baking, remove the bread and put it on a cooling rack.

Calories: 140
Fat: 6 g
Protein: 6 g
Carb: 16 g

15 - Italian Cheese Bread

Servings   14 slices

Difficulty   ● ● ○

Preparation Time   10 m

Cooking Time   2 h

Ingredients

- 1¼ cups water
- 3 cups bread flour
- ½ shredded pepper jack cheese
- 2 teaspoon Italian seasoning
- 2 Tablespoon brown sugar
- 1½ teaspoon salt
- 2 teaspoon active dry yeast

Directions

Add each ingredient to the bread machine in the order and at the temperature recommended by your bread machine manufacturer.

Close the lid, select the basic bread, medium crust setting on your bread machine, and press START.

When the bread machine has finished baking, remove the bread and put it on a cooling rack.

Calories: 130
Fat: 6 g
Protein: 7 g
Carb: 33 g

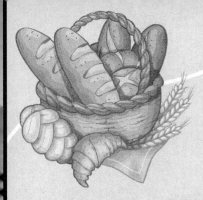

16 - Curd Bread

Servings 14 slices

Difficulty ● ● ○

Preparation Time 15 m

Cooking Time 4 h

Ingredients

- ¾ cup lukewarm water
- 2/3 cups wheat bread machine flour
- ¾ cup cottage cheese
- Tablespoon softened butter
- Tablespoon white sugar
- 1½ teaspoon sea salt
- 1½ Tablespoon sesame seeds
- Tablespoon dried onions
- 1¼ teaspoon bread machine yeast

Directions

Place all the dry and liquid ingredients in the pan and follow the instructions for your bread machine.

Pay particular attention to measuring the ingredients. Use a measuring cup, measuring spoon, and kitchen scales to do so.

Set the baking program to BASIC and the crust type to MEDIUM.
If the dough is too dense or too wet, adjust the amount of flour and liquid in the recipe.

When the program has ended, take the pan out of the bread machine and let cool for 5 minutes.

Shake the loaf out of the pan. If necessary, use a spatula.

Wrap the bread with a kitchen towel and set it aside for an hour. Otherwise, you can cool it on a wire rack.

Calories: 277
Fat: 5 g
Protein: 10 g
Carb: 48 g

17 - Original Italian Herb Bread

Servings 20 slices

Difficulty ● ● ○

Preparation Time 15 m

Cooking Time 3 h

Ingredients

- 1 cup water at 80 degrees F
- ½ cup olive brine
- 1½ tablespoons butter
- 3 tablespoons sugar
- 2 teaspoons salt
- 5 1/3 cups flour
- 2 teaspoons bread machine yeast
- 20 olives, black/green
- 1½ teaspoons Italian herbs

Directions

Cut olives into slices.

Put all ingredients to your bread machine (except olives), carefully following the instructions of the manufacturer.

Set the program of your bread machine to French bread and set crust type to Medium.

Once the maker beeps, add olives.

Wait until the cycle completes.

Once the loaf is ready, take the bucket out and cool the loaf for 6 minutes.

Wobble the bucket to take off the loaf.

Calories: 386
Fat: 7 g
Protein: 10 g
Carb: 65 g

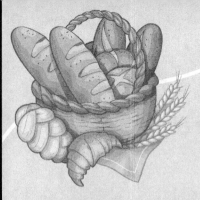

18 - Lovely Aromatic Lavender Bread

Servings   8 slices

Difficulty ● ● ●

Preparation Time   5 m

Cooking Time   2 h 45 m

Ingredients

- ¾ cup milk at 80 degrees F
- 1 tablespoon melted butter, cooled
- 1 tablespoon sugar
- ¾ teaspoon salt
- 1 teaspoon fresh lavender flower, chopped
- ¼ teaspoon lemon zest
- ¼ teaspoon fresh thyme, chopped
- 2 cups white bread flour
- ¾ teaspoon instant yeast

Directions

Add all of the ingredients to your bread machine, carefully following the instructions of the manufacturer.

Set the program of your bread machine to Basic/White Bread and set crust type to Medium.

Wait until the cycle completes.

Once the loaf is ready, take the bucket out and let the loaf cool for 5 minutes. Gently shake the bucket to remove the loaf.

Calories: 144
Fat: 2 g
Protein: 4 g
Carb: 27 g

19 - Cinnamon & Dried Fruits Bread

Servings 16 slices

Difficulty ● ● ●

Preparation Time 5 m

Cooking Time 3 h

Ingredients

- 2¾ cups flour
- 1½ cups dried fruits
- 4 tablespoons sugar
- 2½ tablespoons butter
- 1 tablespoon milk powder
- 1 teaspoon cinnamon
- ½ teaspoon ground nutmeg
- ¼ teaspoon vanillin
- ½ cup peanuts
- powdered sugar, for sprinkling
- 1 teaspoon salt
- 1½ bread machine yeast

Directions

Add all of the ingredients to your bread machine (except peanuts and powdered sugar), carefully following the instructions of the manufacturer.

Set the program of your bread machine to Basic/White Bread and set crust type to Medium.

Once the bread maker beeps, moisten dough with a bit of water and add peanuts.

Wait until the cycle completes.

Once the loaf is ready, take the bucket out and let the loaf cool for 5 minutes.

Gently shake the bucket to remove the loaf.

Sprinkle with powdered sugar.

Calories: 315
Fat: 4 g
Protein: 5 g
Carb: 50 g

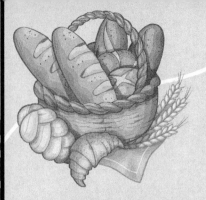

20 - Herbal Garlic Cream Cheese Delight

Servings 8 slices

Difficulty ● ● ○

Preparation Time 5 m

Cooking Time 2 h 45 m

Ingredients

- 1/3 cup water at 80 degrees F
- 1/3 cup herb and garlic cream cheese mix, at room temp
- 1 whole egg, beaten, at room temp
- 4 teaspoons melted butter, cooled
- 1 tablespoon sugar
- 2/3 teaspoon salt
- 2 cups white bread flour
- 1 teaspoon instant yeast

Directions

Add all of the ingredients to your bread machine, carefully following the instructions of the manufacturer.

Set the program of your bread machine to Basic/White Bread and set crust type to Medium.

Wait until the cycle completes.

Once the loaf is ready, take the bucket out and let the loaf cool for 5 minutes.

Gently shake the bucket to remove the loaf.

Calories: 182
Fat: 6 g
Protein: 5 g
Carb: 27 g

21 - Oregano Mozza-Cheese Bread

Servings 16 slices

Difficulty ● ● ○

Preparation Time 15 m

Cooking Time 3 h 15 m

Ingredients

- 1 cup (milk + egg) mixture
- ½ cup mozzarella cheese
- 2¼ cups flour
- ¾ cup whole grain flour
- 2 tablespoons sugar
- 1 teaspoon salt
- 2 teaspoons oregano
- 1½ teaspoons dry yeast

Directions

Add all of the ingredients to your bread machine, carefully following the instructions of the manufacturer.

Set the program of your bread machine to Basic/White Bread and set crust type to Dark.

Wait until the cycle completes.

Once the loaf is ready, take the bucket out and let the loaf cool for 5 minutes.

Gently shake the bucket to remove the loaf.

Calories: 200
Fat: 2 g
Protein: 8 g
Carb: 40 g

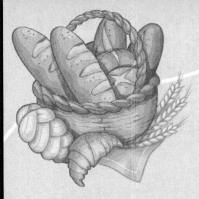

22 - Cumin Tossed Fancy Bread

Servings 16 slices

Difficulty ● ● ○

Preparation Time 5 m

Cooking Time 3 h 15 m

Ingredients

- ·5 1/3 cups wheat flour
- ·1½ teaspoons salt
- ·1½ tablespoons sugar
- ·1 tablespoon dry yeast
- ·1¾ cups water
- ·2 tablespoons cumin
- ·3 tablespoons sunflower oil

Directions

Add warm water to the bread machine bucket.

Add salt, sugar, and sunflower oil.

Sift in wheat flour and add yeast.

Set the program of your bread machine to French bread and set crust type to Medium.

Once the maker beeps, add cumin.

Wait until the cycle completes.

Once the loaf is ready, take the bucket out and let the loaf cool for 5 minutes.

Gently shake the bucket to remove the loaf.

Calories: 368
Fat: 7 g
Protein: 10 g
Carb: 67 g

23 - Potato Rosemary Loaf

Servings 20 slices

Difficulty ● ● ○

Preparation Time 5 m

Cooking Time 3 h 25 m

Ingredients

- ·4 cups wheat flour
- ·1 tablespoon sugar
- ·1 tablespoon sunflower oil
- ·1½ teaspoons salt
- ·1½ cups water
- ·1 teaspoon dry yeast
- ·1 cup mashed potatoes, ground through a sieve
- ·crushed rosemary to taste

Directions

Add flour, salt, and sugar to the bread maker bucket and attach mixing paddle.

Add sunflower oil and water.

Put in yeast as directed.

Set the program of your bread machine to Bread with Filling mode and set crust type to Medium.

Once the bread maker beeps and signals to add more ingredients, open lid, add mashed potatoes, and chopped rosemary.

Wait until the cycle completes.

Once the loaf is ready, take the bucket out and let the loaf cool for 5 minutes.

Gently shake the bucket to remove the loaf.

Calories: 276
Fat: 3 g
Protein: 8 g
Carb: 54 g

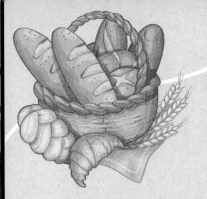

24 - Delicious Honey Lavender Bread

Servings 16 slices

Difficulty ● ● ○

Preparation Time 10 m

Cooking Time 3 h 25 m

Ingredients

- 1½ cups wheat flour
- 2 1/3 cups whole meal flour
- 1 teaspoon fresh yeast
- 1½ cups water
- 1 teaspoon lavender
- 1½ tablespoons honey
- 1 teaspoon salt

Directions

Sift both types of flour in a bowl and mix.

Add all of the ingredients to your bread machine, carefully following the instructions of the manufacturer.

Set the program of your bread machine to Basic/White Bread and set crust type to Medium.

Wait until the cycle completes.

Once the loaf is ready, take the bucket out and let the loaf cool for 5 minutes.

Gently shake the bucket to remove the loaf.

Calories: 226
Fat: 2 g
Protein: 8 g
Carb: 46 g

25 - Inspiring Cinnamon Bread

Servings 8 slices

Difficulty ● ● ○

Preparation Time 15 m

Cooking Time 2 h 15 m

Ingredients

- 2/3 cup milk at 80 degrees F
- 1 whole egg, beaten
- 3 tablespoons melted butter, cooled
- 1/3 cup sugar
- 1/3 teaspoon salt
- 1 teaspoon ground cinnamon
- 2 cups white bread flour
- 1 1/3 teaspoons active dry yeast

Directions

Add all of the ingredients to your bread machine, carefully following the instructions of the manufacturer.

Set the program of your bread machine to Basic/White Bread and set crust type to Medium.

Wait until the cycle completes.

Once the loaf is ready, take the bucket out and let the loaf cool for 5 minutes.

Remove the loaf

Calories: 200
Fat: 5 g
Protein: 5 g
Carb: 34 g

26 - Lavender Buttermilk Bread

Servings 14 slices

Difficulty ● ● ●

Preparation Time 10 m

Cooking Time 3 h

Ingredients

- ½ cup water
- 7/8 cup buttermilk
- 1/4 cup olive oil
- 3 Tablespoon finely chopped fresh lavender leaves
- 1 ¼ teaspoon finely chopped fresh lavender flowers
- Grated zest of 1 lemon
- 4 cups bread flour
- 2 teaspoon salt
- 2 3/4 teaspoon bread machine yeast

Directions

Add each ingredient to the bread machine in the order and at the temperature recommended by your bread machine manufacturer

Close the lid, select the basic bread, medium crust setting on your bread machine and press START.

When the bread machine has finished baking, remove the bread and put it on a cooling rack.

Calories: 170
Fat: 5 g
Protein: 2 g
Carb: 27 g

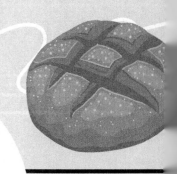

27 - Cajun Bread

Servings 14 slices

Difficulty ● ● ●

Preparation Time 10 m

Cooking Time 2 h

Ingredients

- ½ cup water
- ¼ cup chopped onion
- ¼ cup chopped green bell pepper
- 2 teaspoon finely chopped garlic
- 2 teaspoon soft butter
- 2 cups bread flour
- 1 Tablespoon sugar
- 1 teaspoon Cajun
- ½ teaspoon salt
- 1 teaspoon active dry yeast

Directions

Add each ingredient to the bread machine in the order and at the temperature recommended by your bread machine manufacturer.

Close the lid, select the basic bread, medium crust setting on your bread machine and press START.

When the bread machine has finished baking, remove the bread and put it on a cooling rack.

Calories: 150
Fat: 4 g
Protein: 5 g
Carb: 23 g

28 - Turmeric Bread

Servings   14 slices

Difficulty   ● ● ●

Preparation Time   10 m

Cooking Time   3 h

Ingredients

- 1 teaspoon dried yeast
- 4 cups strong white flour
- 1 teaspoon turmeric powder
- 2 teaspoon beetroot powder
- 2 Tablespoons olive oil
- 1.5 teaspoon salt
- 1 teaspoon chili flakes
- 1 cup water

Directions

Add each ingredient to the bread machine in the order and at the temperature recommended by your bread machine manufacturer.

Close the lid, select the basic bread, medium crust setting on your bread machine and press START.

When the bread machine has finished baking, remove the bread and put it on a cooling rack.

Calories: 150
Fat: 4 g
Protein: 2 g
Carb: 23 g

29 - Rosemary Cranberry Pecan Bread

Servings   14 slices

Difficulty ● ● ●

Preparation Time   30 m

Cooking Time   3 h

Ingredients

- 1 1/3 cups water, plus
- 2 Tablespoon water
- 2 Tablespoon butter
- 2 teaspoon salt
- 4 cups bread flour
- 3/4 cup dried sweetened cranberries
- 3/4 cup toasted chopped pecans
- 2 Tablespoon non-fat powdered milk
- ¼ cup sugar
- 2 teaspoon yeast

Directions

Add each ingredient to the bread machine in the order and at the temperature recommended by your bread machine manufacturer.

Close the lid, select the basic bread, medium crust setting on your bread machine and press START.

When the bread machine has finished baking, remove the bread and put it on a cooling rack.

Calories: 120
Fat: 4 g
Protein: 9 g
Carb: 20 g

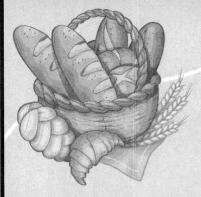

30 - Sesame French Bread

Servings 14 slices

Difficulty ● ● ○

Preparation Time 20 m

Cooking Time 3 h 15 m

Ingredients

- 7/8 cup water
- 1 Tablespoon butter, softened
- 3 cups bread flour
- 2 teaspoon sugar
- 1 teaspoon salt
- 2 teaspoon yeast
- 2 Tablespoon sesame seeds toasted

Directions

Add each ingredient to the bread machine in the order and at the temperature recommended by your bread machine manufacturer.

Close the lid, select the French bread, medium crust setting on your bread machine and press START.

When the bread machine has finished baking, remove the bread and put it on a cooling rack.

Calories: 180
Fat: 3 g
Protein: 6 g
Carb: 28 g

31 - Herb Bread

Servings 1 loaf

Difficulty ● ● ○

Preparation Time 20 m

Cooking Time 1 h 15 m

Ingredients

- 3/4 to 7/8 cup milk
- 1 tablespoon Sugar
- 1 teaspoon Salt
- tablespoon Butter or margarine
- 1/3 cup chopped onion
- cups bread flour
- 1/2 teaspoon Dried dill
- 1/2 teaspoon Dried basil
- 1/2 teaspoon Dried rosemary
- 1/2 teaspoon Active dry yeast

Directions

Place all the Ingredients in the bread pan. Select medium crus then the rapid bake cycle. Press starts.

After 5-10 minutes, observe the dough as it kneads, if you hear straining sounds in your machine or if the dough appears stiff and dry, add 1 tablespoon Liquid at a time until the dough becomes smooth, pliable, soft, and slightly tacky to the touch.

Remove the bread from the pan after baking. Place on rack and allow to cool for 1 hour before slicing.

Calories: 102
Fat: 2 g
Protein: 2 g
Carb: 20 g

32- Original Italian Herb Bread

Servings 2 loaves

Difficulty ● ● ○

Preparation Time 10 m

Cooking Time 50 m

Ingredients

- 1 cup water at 80 degrees F
- ½ cup olive brine
- 1½ tablespoons butter
- tablespoons sugar
- teaspoons salt
- 5⅓ cups flour
- teaspoons bread machine yeast
- 20 olives, black/green
- 1½ teaspoons Italian herbs

Directions

Cut olives into slices.

Add all of the ingredients to your bread machine (except olives), carefully following the instructions of the manufacturer.

Set the program of your bread machine to French bread and set crust type to Medium. Press START.

Once the maker beeps, add olives.

Wait until the cycle completes.

Once the loaf is ready, take the bucket out and let the loaf cool for 5 minutes. Gently shake the bucket to remove the loaf.

Transfer to a cooling rack, slice, and serve.

Calories: 132
Fat: 7 g
Protein: 10 g
Carb: 71 g

33 - Cumin Bread

Servings 10 slices

Difficulty ● ● ●

Preparation Time 15 m

Cooking Time 3 h 15 m

Ingredients

1 teaspoon bread machine yeast

2½ cups wheat bread machine flour

1 Tablespoon panifarin

1½ teaspoon kosher salt

1½ Tablespoon white sugar

Tablespoon extra-virgin olive oil

Tablespoon tomatoes, dried and chopped

1 Tablespoon tomato paste

½ cup firm cheese (cubes)

½ cup feta cheese

1 pinch saffron

1½ cups serum

Directions

Five minutes before cooking, pour in dried tomatoes and 1 tablespoon of olive oil. Add the tomato paste and mix.

Place all the dry and liquid ingredients, except additives, in the pan and follow the instructions for your bread machine. Pay particular attention to measuring the ingredients. Use a measuring cup, measuring spoon, and kitchen scales to do so.

Set the baking program to BASIC and the crust type to MEDIUM.

Add the additives after the beep or place them in the dispenser of the bread machine.

Shake the loaf out of the pan. If necessary, use a spatula.

Wrap the bread with a kitchen towel and set it aside for an hour. Otherwise, you can cool it on a wire rack.

Calories: 268
Fat: 9 g
Protein: 10 g
Carb: 37 g

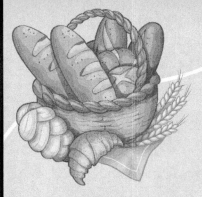

34 - Saffron Tomato Bread

Servings 8 slices

Difficulty ●○○

Preparation Time 15 m

Cooking Time 3 h 30 m

Ingredients

- 1/3 cups bread machine flour, sifted
- 1½ teaspoon kosher salt
- 1½ Tablespoon sugar
- 1 Tablespoon bread machine yeast
- 1¾ cups lukewarm water
- Tablespoon black cumin
- Tablespoon sunflower oil

Directions

Place all the dry and liquid ingredients in the pan and follow the instructions for your bread machine.

Set the baking program to BASIC and the crust type to MEDIUM.

If the dough is too dense or too wet, adjust the amount of flour and liquid in the recipe.

When the program has ended, take the pan out of the bread machine and let cool for 5 minutes.

Shake the loaf out of the pan. If necessary, use a spatula.

Wrap the bread with a kitchen towel and set it aside for an hour. Otherwise, you can cool it on a wire rack.

Calories: 388
Fat: 7 g
Protein: 10 g
Carb: 67 g

35 - Peaches and Cream Bread

Servings 12-16 slices

Difficulty ● ○ ○

Preparation Time 15 m

Cooking Time 2 h 3 m

Ingredients

- Butter for greasing the bucket
- 1½ cups pumpkin purée
- eggs, at room temperature
- ⅓ cup melted butter, cooled
- 1 cup sugar
- cups all-purpose flour
- 1½ teaspoons baking powder
- ¾ teaspoon ground cinnamon
- ½ teaspoon baking soda
- ¼ teaspoon ground nutmeg
- ¼ teaspoon ground ginger
- ¼ teaspoon salt
- Pinch ground cloves

Directions

Lightly grease the bread bucket with butter.

Add the pumpkin, eggs, butter, and sugar.

Program the machine for Quick/Rapid bread and press START.

Let the wet ingredients be mixed by the paddles until the first fast mixing cycle is finished, about 10 minutes into the cycle.

When the loaf is done, remove the bucket from the machine.

Let the loaf cool for 5 minutes.

Gently shake the bucket to remove the loaf, and turn it out onto a rack to cool.

Calories: 251
Fat: 7 g
Protein: 5 g
Carb: 43 g

71

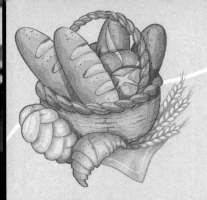

36 - Warm Spiced Pumpkin Bread

Servings 8 slices

Difficulty ● ○ ○

Preparation Time 15 m

Cooking Time 2 h

Ingredients

- ½ cup canned peaches, drained and chopped
- ¼ cup heavy whipping cream, at 80°F to 90°F
- 1 egg, at room temperature
- ¾ tablespoon melted butter, cooled
- 1½ tablespoons sugar
- ¾ teaspoon salt
- ¼ teaspoon ground cinnamon
- ⅛ teaspoon ground nutmeg
- ¼ cup whole-wheat flour
- 1¾ cups white bread flour
- ¾ teaspoons bread machine or instant yeast

Directions

Place the ingredients in your bread machine as recommended by the manufacturer.

Program the machine for Basic/White bread, select light or medium crust, and press START.

When the loaf is done, remove the bucket from the machine.

Let the loaf cool for 5 minutes.

Gently shake the bucket to remove the loaf, and turn it out onto a rack to cool.

Calories: 153
Fat: 7 g
Protein: 10 g
Carb: 27 g

37 - Pure Peach Bread

Servings 12 slices

Difficulty ● ○ ○

Preparation Time 15 m

Cooking Time 2 h

Ingredients

¾ cup peaches, chopped

⅓ cup heavy whipping cream

1 egg

1 tablespoon butter, melted at room temperature

⅓ teaspoon ground cinnamon

⅛ teaspoon ground nutmeg

¼ tablespoons sugar

1 ⅛ teaspoons salt

⅓ cup whole-wheat flour

⅔ cups white bread flour

1 ⅛ teaspoons instant or bread machine yeast

Directions

Take 1 ½ pound size loaf pan and first add the liquid ingredients and then add the dry ingredients.

Place the loaf pan in the machine and close its top lid.

For selecting a bread cycle, press "Basic Bread/White Bread/Regular Bread" and for selecting a crust type, press "Light" or "Medium".
START preparing the bread.

After the bread loaf is completed, open the lid and take out the loaf pan.

Allow the pan to cool down for 10-15 minutes on a wire rack.
Gently shake the pan and remove the bread loaf.

Make slices and serve.

Calories: 153
Fat: 7 g
Protein: 10 g
Carb: 27 g

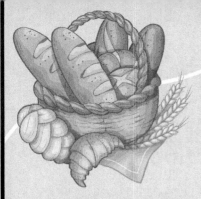

Servings 12 slices

Difficulty ● ○ ○

Preparation Time 15 m

Cooking Time 2 h

Ingredients

- ¾ cup milk, lukewarm
- 1 egg, at room temperature
- ¼ tablespoons butter, melted at room temperature
- 1 ½ tablespoons honey
- ½ cup rolled oats
- ⅓ cups white bread flour
- 1 ⅛ teaspoons salt
- 1 ½ teaspoons instant or bread machine yeast
- ½ cup dried blueberries

Directions

Take 1 ½ pound size loaf pan and first add the liquid ingredients and then add the dry ingredients. (Do not add the blueberries as of now.)

Place the loaf pan in the machine and close its top lid.

Plug the bread machine into power socket. For selecting a bread cycle, press "Basic Bread/White Bread/Regular Bread" or "Fruit/Nut Bread" and for selecting a crust type, press "Light" or "Medium". START the machine.

When machine beeps or signals, add the blueberries.

After the bread loaf is completed, open the lid and take out the loaf pan.

Allow the pan to cool down for 10-15 minutes on a wire rack.

Gently shake the pan and remove the bread loaf.

Calories: 153
Fat: 7 g
Protein: 10 g
Carb: 27 g

39 - Sunflower & Flax Seed Bread

Servings   10 slices

Difficulty ● ○ ○

Preparation Time 5 m

Cooking Time 3 h

Ingredients

- Water – 1 1/3 cups.
- Butter – 2 tablespoons.
- Honey – 3 tablespoons.
- Bread flour – 1 ½ cups.
- Whole wheat flour – 1 1/3 cups.
- Salt – 1 teaspoon.
- Active dry yeast – 1 teaspoon.
- Flax seeds – ½ cup.
- Sunflower seeds – ½ cup.

Directions

Add all ingredients except for sunflower seeds into the bread machine pan.

Select basic setting then select light/medium crust and press START.

Add sunflower seeds just before the final kneading cycle.

Once loaf is done, remove the loaf pan from the machine. Allow it to cool for 10 minutes. Slice and serve.

Calories: 220
Fat: 7 g
Protein: 4 g
Carb: 36 g

40 - Nutritious 9-Grain Bread

Servings   10 slices

Difficulty ● ● ○

Preparation Time 5 m

Cooking Time 2 h

Ingredients

- Warm water – 3/4 cup+2 tablespoons.
- Whole wheat flour – 1 cup.
- Bread flour – 1 cup.
- 9-grain cereal – ½ cup., crushed
- Salt – 1 teaspoon.
- Butter – 1 tablespoon.
- Sugar – 2 tablespoons.
- Milk powder – 1 tablespoon.
- Active dry yeast – 2 teaspoons.

Directions

Put all ingredients into the bread machine.

Select whole wheat setting then select light/medium crust and START.

Once loaf is done, remove the loaf pan from the machine.

Allow it to cool for 10 minutes.

Slice and serve.

Calories: 132
Fat: 2 g
Protein: 4 g
Carb: 25 g

41- Oatmeal Sunflower Bread

Servings   10 slices

Difficulty ● ● ○

Preparation Time 15 m

Cooking Time 3 h 30 m

Ingredients

- Water – 1 cup.
- Honey – ¼ cup.
- Butter – 2 tablespoons., softened
- Bread flour – 3 cups.
- Old fashioned oats – ½ cup.
- Milk powder – 2 tablespoons.
- Salt – 1 ¼ teaspoons.
- Active dry yeast – 2 ¼ teaspoons.
- Sunflower seeds – ½ cup.

Directions

Add all ingredients except for sunflower seeds into the bread machine pan.

Select basic setting then select light/medium crust and press START. Add sunflower seeds just before the final kneading cycle.

Once loaf is done, remove the loaf pan from the machine. Allow it to cool for 10 minutes. Slice and serve.

Calories: 215
Fat: 4 g
Protein: 5 g
Carb: 40 g

42 - Cornmeal Whole Wheat Bread

Servings 10 slices

Difficulty ● ● ○

Preparation Time 15 m

Cooking Time 2 h

Ingredients

- Active dry yeast – 2 ½ teaspoons.
- Water – 1 1/3 cups.
- Sugar – 2 tablespoons.
- Egg – 1, lightly beaten
- Butter – 2 tablespoons.
- Salt – 1 ½ teaspoons.
- Cornmeal – 3/4 cup.
- Whole wheat flour – 3/4 cup.
- Bread flour – 2 3/4 cups.

Directions

Add all ingredients to the bread machine pan according to the bread machine manufacturer instructions.

Select basic bread setting then select medium crust and START.

Once loaf is done, remove the loaf pan from the machine.

Allow it to cool for 10 minutes. Slice and serve.

Calories: 228
Fat: 6 g
Protein: 5 g
Carb: 41 g

43 - Delicious Cranberry Bread

Servings   10 slices

Difficulty ● ● ○

Preparation Time 5 m

Cooking Time 3 h 30 m

Ingredients

- Warm water – 1 ½ cups
- Brown sugar – 2 tablespoons.
- Salt – 1 ½ teaspoons.
- Olive oil – 2 tablespoons.
- Flour – 4 cups
- Cinnamon – 1 ½ teaspoons.
- Cardamom – 1 ½ teaspoons.
- Dried cranberries – 1 cup
- Yeast – 2 teaspoons.

Directions

Put all ingredients to the bread machine in the listed order.

Select sweet bread setting then select light/medium crust and START.

Once loaf is done, remove the loaf pan from the machine.

Allow it to cool for 20 minutes. Slice and serve.

Calories: 228
Fat: 3 g
Protein: 5 g
Carb: 41 g

44 - Coffee Raisin Bread

Servings   10 slices

Difficulty ● ○ ○

Preparation Time 10 m

Cooking Time 3 h

Ingredients

- Active dry yeast – 2 ½ teaspoons.
- Ground cloves – ¼ teaspoon.
- Ground allspice – ¼ teaspoon.
- Ground cinnamon – 1 teaspoon.
- Sugar – 3 tablespoons.
- Egg – 1, lightly beaten
- Olive oil – 3 tablespoons.
- Strong brewed coffee – 1 cup.
- Bread flour – 3 cups.
- Raisins – 3/4 cup.
- Salt – 1 ½ teaspoons.

Directions

Put all ingredients to the bread machine in the listed order.

Select sweet bread setting then select light/medium crust and START.

Once loaf is done, remove the loaf pan from the machine.

Allow it to cool for 20 minutes. Slice and serve.

Calories: 228
Fat: 3 g
Protein: 5 g
Carb: 41 g

45 - Healthy Multigrain Bread

Servings 10 slices

Difficulty ● ○ ○

Preparation Time 5 m

Cooking Time 40 m

Ingredients

- Water – 1 ¼ cups.
- Butter – 2 tablespoons.
- Bread flour – 1 1/3 cups.
- Whole wheat flour – 1 ½ cups.
- Multigrain cereal – 1 cup.
- Brown sugar – 3 tablespoons.
- Salt – 1 ¼ teaspoons.
- Yeast – 2 ½ teaspoons.

Directions

Put ingredients listed into the bread machine pan. Select basic bread, setting then select light/medium crust and START.

Once loaf is done, remove the loaf pan from the machine.
Allow it to cool for 10 minutes.

Slice and serve.

Calories: 228
Fat: 3 g
Protein: 5 g
Carb: 41 g

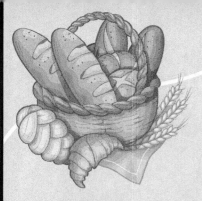

46 - Italian Pine Nut Bread

Servings   10 slices

Difficulty ●○○

Preparation Time   5 m

Cooking Time   3 h 30 m

Ingredients

- Water – 1 cup+ 2 tablespoons.
- Bread flour – 3 cups.
- Sugar – 2 tablespoons.
- Salt – 1 teaspoon.
- Active dry yeast – 1 1/4 teaspoons.
- Basil pesto – 1/3 cup.
- Flour – 2 tablespoons.
- Pine nuts – 1/3 cup.

Directions

In a small container, combine basil pesto and flour and mix until well blended. Add pine nuts and stir well. Add water, bread flour, sugar, salt, and yeast into the bread machine pan.

Select basic setting then select medium crust and press START.

Add basil pesto mixture just before the final kneading cycle.

Once loaf is done, remove the loaf pan from the machine.
Allow it to cool for 10 minutes.

Slice and serve.

Calories: 180
Fat: 4 g
Protein: 5 g
Carb: 32 g

47 - Whole Wheat Raisin Bread

Servings 10 slices

Difficulty ●○○

Preparation Time 5 m

Cooking Time 2 h

Ingredients

- Whole wheat flour – 3 ½ cups
- Dry yeast – 2 teaspoons.
- Eggs – 2, lightly beaten
- Butter – ¼ cup, softened
- Water – 3/4 cup
- Milk – 1/3 cup
- Salt – 1 teaspoon.
- Sugar – 1/3 cup
- Cinnamon – 4 teaspoons.
- Raisins – 1 cup

Directions

Add water, milk, butter, and eggs to the bread pan. Add remaining ingredients except for yeast to the bread pan.

Make a small hole into the flour with your finger and add yeast to the hole. Make sure yeast will not be mixed with any liquids.

Select whole wheat setting then select light/medium crust and START. Once loaf is done, remove the loaf pan from the machine.

Allow it to cool for 10 minutes.

Slice and serve.

Calories: 180
Fat: 4 g
Protein: 5 g
Carb: 32 g

48 - Healthy Spelt Bread

Servings 10 slices

Difficulty ● ○ ○

Preparation Time 15 m

Cooking Time 40 m

Ingredients

- Milk – 1 ¼ cups.
- Sugar – 2 tablespoons.
- Olive oil – 2 tablespoons.
- Salt – 1 teaspoon.
- Spelt flour – 4 cups.
- Yeast – 2 ½ teaspoons.

Directions

Add all ingredients according to the bread machine manufacturer instructions into the bread machine.

Select basic bread setting then select light/medium crust and START.

Once loaf is done, remove the loaf pan from the machine.

Allow it to cool for 10 minutes.

Slice and serve.

Calories: 223
Fat: 4 g
Protein: 9 g
Carb: 40 g

49 - Awesome Rosemary Bread

Servings   8 slices

Difficulty ● ○ ○

Preparation Time 5 m

Cooking Time 2 h

Ingredients

- 3/4 cup + 1 tablespoon water at 80 degrees F
- 1 2/3 tablespoons melted butter, cooled
- 2 teaspoons sugar
- 1 teaspoon salt
- 1 tablespoon fresh rosemary, chopped
- 2 cups white bread flour
- 1+1/3 teaspoons instant yeast

Directions

Combine all of the ingredients to your bread machine, carefully following the instructions of the manufacturer.

Set the program of your bread machine to Basic/White Bread and set crust type to Medium.

Press START.

Wait until the cycle completes.

Once the loaf is ready, take the bucket out and allow the loaf to chill for 5 minutes.

Gently jiggle the bucket to take out the loaf.

Calories: 140
Fat: 1 g
Protein: 4 g
Carb: 25 g

50 - Herbed Baguette

Servings   12 slices

Difficulty ● ● ●

Preparation Time   10 m

Cooking Time   45 m

Ingredients

- 1 1/4 cups warm water
- cups sourdough starter, either fed or unfed
- to 5 cups all-purpose flour
- 1/2 teaspoons salt
- teaspoons sugar
- 1 tablespoon instant yeast
- 1 tablespoon fresh oregano, chopped
- 1 teaspoon fresh rosemary, chopped
- 1 tablespoon fresh basil, chopped
- any other desired herbs

Directions

In the bowl of a stand mixer, combine all ingredients, knead with a dough hook (or use your hands) until smooth dough forms -- about 10 minutes, if needed, add more flour.

Place the dough in an oiled bowl, cover, and allow to rise for about 2 hours.

Punch down the dough, and divide it into 3 pieces. Shape each piece of dough into a baguette -- about 16 inches long. You can do this by rolling the dough into a log, folding it, rolling it into a log, then folding it and rolling it again.

Place the rolled baguette dough onto lined baking sheets, and cover. Let rise for one hour.

Preheat oven to 425F, and bake for 20-25 minutes.

Calories: 197
Fat: 1 g
Protein: 7 g
Carb: 38 g

51 - Pumpernickel Bread

Servings   1 loaf

Difficulty ● ● ●

Preparation Time 50 m

Cooking Time 2 h 10 m

Ingredients

- 1 1/8 cups warm water
- 1 ½ tablespoons vegetable oil
- 1/3 cup molasses
- tablespoons cocoa
- 1 tablespoon caraway seed (optional)
- 1 ½ teaspoon salt
- 1 ½ cups of bread flour
- 1 cup of rye flour
- 1 cup whole wheat flour
- 1 ½ tablespoons of vital wheat gluten (optional)
- ½ teaspoon of bread machine yeast

Calories: 97
Fat: 1 g
Protein: 3 g
Carb: 19 g

Directions

Add all ingredients to bread machine pan.

Choose basic bread cycle.

Take bread out to cool and enjoy!

52 - Honey Sourdough Bread

Servings 1 loaf

Difficulty ● ○ ○

Preparation Time 15 m

Cooking Time 3 h

Ingredients

- 2/3 cup sourdough starter
- 1/2 cup water
- 1 tablespoon vegetable oil
- 2 tablespoons honey
- 1/2 teaspoon salt
- 1/2 cup high protein wheat flour
- 2 cups bread flour
- 1 teaspoon active dry yeast

Directions

Measure 1 cup of starter and remaining bread ingredients, add to bread machine pan.

Choose basic/white bread cycle with medium or light crust color.

Calories: 177
Fat: 1 g
Protein: 3 g
Carb: 33 g

53 - Multigrain Sourdough Bread

Servings 1 loaf

Difficulty ● ○ ○

Preparation Time 15 m

Cooking Time 3 h

Ingredients

- 2 cups sourdough starter
- 2 tablespoons butter or 2 tablespoons olive oil
- 1/2 cup milk
- 1 teaspoon salt
- 1/4 cup honey
- 1/2 cup sunflower seeds
- 1/2 cup millet or 1/2 cup amaranth or 1/2 cup quinoa
- 3 1/2 cups multi-grain flour

Directions

Add ingredients to bread machine pan.

Choose dough cycle.

Conventional Oven:
When cycle is over, take out dough and place on lightly floured surface and shape into loaf.

Place in greased loaf pan, cover, and rise until bread is a couple inches above the edge.

For 40 to 50 minutes, Bake at 375 F degrees.

Calories: 110
Fat: 1 g
Protein: 3 g
Carb: 23 g

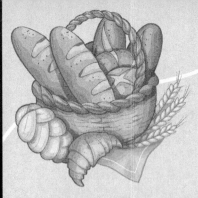

54 - Olive and Garlic Sourdough Bread

Servings 1 loaf

Difficulty ● ○ ○

Preparation Time 15 m

Cooking Time 3 h

Ingredients

- 2 cups sourdough starter
- 3 cups flour
- 2 tablespoons olive oil
- 2 tablespoons sugar
- 2 teaspoon salt
- 1/2 cup chopped black olives
- 6 cloves chopped garlic

Directions

Add starter and bread ingredients to bread machine pan.
Choose dough cycle.

Conventional Oven:
Preheat oven to 350 degrees.
When cycle is complete, if dough is sticky add more flour.

Shape dough onto baking sheet or put into loaf pan

Bake for 35- 45 minutes until golden

Cool before slicing.

Calories: 150
Fat: 1 g
Protein: 3 g
Carb: 26 g

55 - Herbed Baguette

Servings 12 slices

Difficulty ● ○ ○

Preparation Time 30 m

Cooking Time 45 m

Ingredients

- 1 1/4 cups warm water
- 2 cups sourdough starter, either fed or unfed
- 4 to 5 cups all-purpose flour
- 2 1/2 teaspoons salt
- 2 teaspoons sugar
- 1 tablespoon instant yeast
- 1 tablespoon fresh oregano, chopped
- 1 teaspoon fresh rosemary, chopped
- 1 tablespoon fresh basil, chopped
- Any other desired herbs

Calories: 200
Fat: 1 g
Protein: 5 g
Carb: 37 g

Directions

In the bowl of a mixer, combine all the ingredients, knead with a dough hook (or use your hands) until a smooth dough is formed - about 7 to 10 minutes, if necessary, add more flour.
Oil a bowl and place the dough, cover and let it rest for about 2 hours.

Beat the dough and divide it into 3 parts. Form each piece of dough into a loaf of bread, about 16 inches long. You can do this by rolling the dough into a trunk, folding it, rolling it into a trunk and then folding it again.

Place the rolled baguette dough onto lined baking sheets, and cover.
Let rise for one hour.
Preheat oven to 425F, and bake for 20-25 minutes

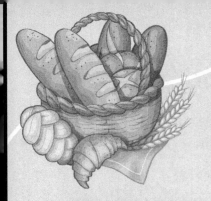

56 - Sauerkraut Rye

Servings   1 loaf

Difficulty ●　○　○

Preparation Time   30 m

Cooking Time   2 h 20 m

Ingredients

- 1 cup sauerkraut, rinsed and drained
- 3/4 cup warm water
- 1½ tablespoons molasses
- 1½ tablespoons butter
- 1½ tablespoons brown sugar
- 1 teaspoon caraway seeds
- 1½ teaspoons salt
- 1 cup rye flour
- 2 cups bread flour
- 1½ teaspoons active dry yeast

Directions

Add all of the ingredients to your bread machine.

Set the program of your bread machine to Basic/White Bread and set crust type to Medium
Wait until the cycle completes.

Once the loaf is ready, take the bucket out and let the loaf cool for 5 minutes.

Gently shake the bucket to take out the loaf

Calories: 74
Fat: 1 g
Protein: 2 g
Carb: 12 g

57 - French Sourdough Bread

Servings 1 loaf

Difficulty ● ○ ○

Preparation Time 15 m

Cooking Time 3 h

Ingredients

- 2 cups sourdough starter
- 1 teaspoon salt
- 1/2 cup water
- 4 cups white bread flour
- 2 tablespoons white cornmeal

Directions

Add ingredients to bread machine pan, saving cornmeal for later.

Choose dough cycle.

Conventional Oven:

Preheat oven to 375 degrees.

At end of dough cycle, place dough onto a surface that is floured.

Add flour if dough is sticky.

Divide dough into 2 portions and flatten into an oval shape 1 ½ inch thick.

Fold ovals in half lengthwise and pinch seams to elongate.

Sprinkle cornmeal onto baking sheet and place the loaves seam side down.

Cover and let rise in until about doubled.

Place a deep pan of hot water on the bottom shelf of the oven;

Use a knife to make shallow, diagonal slashes in tops of loaves

Place the loaves in the oven and sprinkle with fine water mister. Spray the oven walls as well.

Repeat spraying 3 times at one minute intervals.

Remove pan of water after 15 minutes of baking

Fully bake for 30 to 40 minutes or until golden brown.

Calories: 754
Fat: 1 g
Protein: 26 g
Carb: 192 g

58 - Sourdough Starter

Servings 1 loaf

Difficulty ● ○ ○

Preparation Time 5 days

Ingredients

- 2 cups warm water
- 1 tablespoon sugar
- 1 active dry yeast
- 2 cups flour
- 1 proper container
- 1 spoon for stirring

Directions

Day 1:

Combine the water, yeast, and sugar in a medium bowl, and whisk to combine. Gently stir in the flour until well combined, and transfer to your container. Let it sit, loosely covered, in a warm spot for 24 hours.

Day 2 - 4

Unlike the traditional starter, you don't need to feed this one yet. Stir it once or twice every 24 hours.

Day 5:

By now the starter should have developed the classic slightly sour smell. If not, don't worry; you just need to let it sit a bit longer. If it is ready, store it in the fridge, and feed it once a week until you're ready to use it. As with the traditional starter, you'll need to feed it the day before you plan to use it.

Calories: 74
Fat: 1 g
Protein: 2 g
Carb: 12 g

59 - Mom's White Bread

Servings 16 slices

Difficulty ● ○ ○

Preparation Time 5 m

Cooking Time 3 h

Ingredients

- 1 cup and 3 Tablespoon water
- 2 Tablespoon vegetable oil
- 1½ teaspoon salt
- 2 Tablespoon sugar
- 3¼ cups white bread flour
- 2 teaspoon active dry yeast

Directions

Add each ingredient to the bread machine in the order and at the temperature recommended by your bread machine manufacturer.

Close the lid, select the basic or white bread, medium crust setting on your bread machine, and press START.

When the bread machine has finished baking, remove the bread and put it on a cooling rack.

Calories: 104
Fat: 2 g
Protein: 5 g
Carb: 24 g

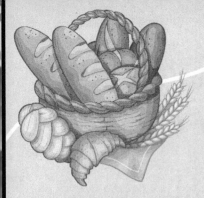

60 - Vegan White Bread

Servings   14 slices

Difficulty ● ● ○

Preparation Time 5 m

Cooking Time 3 h

Ingredients

- 1 1/3 cups water
- 1/3 cup plant milk (I use silk soy original)
- 1½ teaspoon salt
- 2 Tablespoon granulated sugar
- 2 Tablespoon vegetable oil
- 3½ cups all-purpose flour
- 1¾ teaspoon bread machine yeast

Directions

Add each ingredient to the bread machine in the order and at the temperature recommended by your bread machine manufacturer.

Close the lid, select the basic or white bread, medium crust setting on your bread machine, and press START.

When the bread machine has finished baking, remove the bread and put it on a cooling rack.

Calories: 80
Fat: 2 g
Protein: 5 g
Carb: 12 g

61 - Rice Flour Rice Bread

Servings 16 slices

Difficulty ● ● ○

Preparation Time 10 m

Cooking Time 3 h 15 m

Ingredients

3 eggs

1½ cups water

3 Tablespoon vegetable oil

1 teaspoon apple cider vinegar

2¼ teaspoon active dry yeast

3¼ cups white rice flour

2½ teaspoon xanthan gum

1½ teaspoon salt

½ cup dry milk powder

3 Tablespoon white sugar

Directions

In a medium-size bowl, add the oil, water, eggs, and vinegar.
In a large dish, add the yeast, salt, xanthan gum, dry milk powder, rice flour, and sugar.

Mix with a whisk until incorporated.
Add each ingredient to the bread machine in the order and at the temperature recommended by your bread machine manufacturer.

Close the lid, select the whole wheat, medium crust setting on your bread machine, and press START.

When the bread machine has finished baking, remove the bread and put it on a cooling rack.

Calories: 80
Fat: 2 g
Protein: 2 g
Carb: 21 g

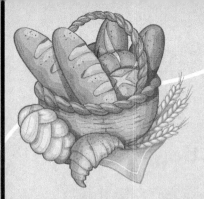

62 - Italian White Bread

Servings 16 slices

Difficulty ● ○ ○

Preparation Time 5 m

Cooking Time 3 h

Ingredients

- ¾ cup cold water
- 2 cups bread flour
- 1 Tablespoon sugar
- 1 teaspoon salt
- 1 Tablespoon olive oil
- 1 teaspoon active dry yeast

Directions

Add each ingredient to the bread machine in the order and at the temperature recommended by your bread machine manufacturer.

Close the lid, select the Italian or basic bread, low crust setting on your bread machine, and press START.

When the bread machine has finished baking, remove the bread and put it on a cooling rack.

Calories: 80
Fat: 2 g
Protein: 2 g
Carb: 11 g

63 - Anadama White Bread

Servings 14 slices

Difficulty ● ○ ○

Preparation Time 5 m

Cooking Time 3 h

Ingredients

- 1 1/8 cups water (110°F)
- 1/3 cup molasses
- 1½ Tablespoon butter at room temperature
- 1 teaspoon salt
- 1/3 cup yellow cornmeal
- 3½ cups bread flour
- 2½ teaspoon bread machine yeast

Directions

Add each ingredient to the bread machine in the order and at the temperature recommended by your bread machine manufacturer.

Close the lid, select the basic bread, low crust setting on your bread machine, and press START.

When the bread machine has finished baking, remove the bread and put it on a cooling rack.

Calories: 80
Fat: 2 g
Protein: 2 g
Carb: 19 g

64 - Soft White Bread

Servings 14 slices

Difficulty ● ○ ○

Preparation Time 5 m

Cooking Time 3 h

Ingredients

- 2 cups water
- 4 teaspoon yeast
- 6 Tablespoon sugar
- ½ cup vegetable oil
- 2 teaspoon salt
- 3 cups strong white flour

Directions

Add each ingredient to the bread machine in the order and at the temperature recommended by your bread machine manufacturer.

Close the lid, select the basic bread, low crust setting on your bread machine, and press START.

When the bread machine has finished baking, remove the bread and put it on a cooling rack.

Calories: 74
Fat: 2 g
Protein: 2 g
Carb: 18 g

65 - English Muffin Bread

Servings 14 slices

Difficulty ● ○ ○

Preparation Time 5 m

Cooking Time 3 h 40 m

Ingredients

- 1 teaspoon vinegar
- 1/4 to 1/3 cup water
- 1 cup lukewarm milk
- 2 Tablespoon butter or 2 Tablespoon vegetable oil
- 1½ teaspoon salt
- 1½ teaspoon sugar
- ½ teaspoon baking powder
- 3½ cups unbleached all-purpose flour
- 2 1/4 teaspoon instant yeast

Directions

Add each ingredient to the bread machine in the order and at the temperature recommended by your bread machine manufacturer.

Close the lid, select the basic bread, low crust setting on your bread machine, and press START.

When the bread machine has finished baking, remove the bread and put it on a cooling rack.

Calories: 62
Fat: 2 g
Protein: 2 g
Carb: 13 g

66 - Cranberry Orange Breakfast Bread

Servings   14 slices

Difficulty ● ○ ○

Preparation Time   5 m

Cooking Time   3 h 10 m

Ingredients

- 1 1/8 cup orange juice
- 2 Tablespoon vegetable oil
- 2 Tablespoon honey
- 3 cups bread flour
- 1 Tablespoon dry milk powder
- ½ teaspoon ground cinnamon
- ½ teaspoon ground allspice
- 1 teaspoon salt
- 1 (.25 ounce) package active dry yeast
- 1 Tablespoon grated orange zest
- 1 cup sweetened dried cranberries
- 1/3 cup chopped walnuts

Directions

Add each ingredient to the bread machine in the order and at the temperature recommended by your bread machine manufacturer.

Close the lid, select the basic bread, low crust setting on your bread machine, and press START.

Add the cranberries and chopped walnuts 5 to 10 minutes before last kneading cycle ends.

When the bread machine has finished baking, remove the bread and put it on a cooling rack.

Calories: 56
Fat: 2 g
Protein: 9 g
Carb: 29 g

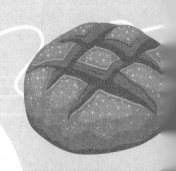

67 - Buttermilk Honey Bread

Servings 14 slices

Difficulty ● ● ○

Preparation Time 5 m

Cooking Time 3 h 45 m

Ingredients

- ½ cup water
- ¾ cup buttermilk
- ¼ cup honey
- 3 Tablespoon butter, softened and cut into pieces
- 3 cups bread flour
- 1½ teaspoon salt
- 2¼ teaspoon yeast (or 1 package)

Directions

Add each ingredient to the bread machine in the order and at the temperature recommended by your bread machine manufacturer.

Close the lid, select the basic bread, medium crust setting on your bread machine and press START.

When the bread machine has finished baking, remove the bread and put it on a cooling rack.

Calories: 92
Fat: 2 g
Protein: 2 g
Carb: 19 g

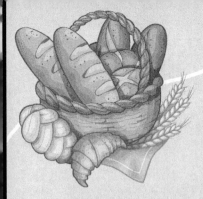

68 - Whole Wheat Breakfast Bread

Servings 14 slices

Difficulty ● ○ ○

Preparation Time 5 m

Cooking Time 3 h 45 m

Ingredients

- 3 cups white whole wheat flour
- ½ teaspoon salt
- 1 cup water
- ½ cup coconut oil, liquified
- 4 Tablespoon honey
- 2½ teaspoon active dry yeast

Directions

Add each ingredient to the bread machine in the order and at the temperature recommended by your bread machine manufacturer.

Close the lid, select the basic bread, medium crust setting on your bread machine and press START.

When the bread machine has finished baking, remove the bread and put it on a cooling rack.

Calories: 60
Fat: 2 g
Protein: 2 g
Carb: 11 g

69 - Cinnamon-Raisin Bread

Servings 10 slices

Difficulty ●○○

Preparation Time 5 m

Cooking Time 3 h

Ingredients

- 1 cup water
- 2 Tablespoon butter, softened
- 3 cups Gold Medal Better for Bread flour
- 3 Tablespoon sugar
- 1½ teaspoon salt
- 1 teaspoon ground cinnamon
- 2½ teaspoon bread machine yeast
- ¾ cup raisins

Directions

Add each ingredient except the raisins to the bread machine in the order and at the temperature recommended by your bread machine manufacturer.

Close the lid, select the sweet or basic bread, medium crust setting on your bread machine and press START.

Add raisins 10 minutes before the last kneading cycle ends.

When the bread machine has finished baking, remove the bread and put it on a cooling rack.

Calories: 182
Fat: 2 g
Protein: 2 g
Carb: 35 g

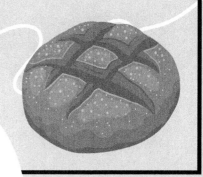

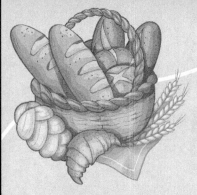

70 - Butter Bread Rolls

Servings 10 slices

Difficulty ● ○ ○

Preparation Time 5 m

Cooking Time 3 h

Ingredients

- 1 cup warm milk
- 1/2 cup butter or 1/2 cup margarine, softened
- 1/4 cup sugar
- 2 eggs
- 1 1/2 teaspoons salt
- 4 cups bread flour
- 2 1/4 teaspoons active dry yeast

Directions

In bread machine pan, put all ingredients in order suggested by manufacturer.
Select dough setting.

When cycle is completed, turn dough onto a lightly floured surface.

Divide dough into 24 portions.
Shape dough into balls.

Place in a greased 13 inch by 9-inch baking pan.

Cover and let rise in a warm place for 30-45 minutes.

Bake at 350 F degrees for 13-16 minutes or until golden brown.

Calories: 182
Fat: 2 g
Protein: 4 g
Carb: 38 g

71 - Cranberry & Golden Raisin Bread

Servings 14 slices

Difficulty ● ○ ○

Preparation Time 5 m

Cooking Time 3 h

Ingredients

- 1 1/3 cups water
- 4 Tablespoon sliced butter
- 3 cups flour
- 1 cup old fashioned oatmeal
- 1/3 cup brown sugar
- 1 teaspoon salt
- 4 Tablespoon dried cranberries
- 4 Tablespoon golden raisins
- 2 teaspoon bread machine yeast

Directions

Add each ingredient except cranberries and golden raisins to the bread machine one by one, according to the manufacturer's instructions.

Close the lid, select the sweet or basic bread, medium crust setting on your bread machine and press START.

Add the cranberries and golden raisins 5 to 10 minutes before the last kneading cycle ends.

When the bread machine has finished baking, remove the bread and put it on a cooling rack.

Calories: 182
Fat: 2 g
Protein: 4 g
Carb: 33 g

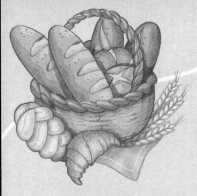

72 - Brown & White Sugar Bread

Servings 12 slices

Difficulty ● ○ ○

Preparation Time 5 m

Cooking Time 3 h

Ingredients

- 1 cup milk (room temperature)
- ¼ cup butter, softened
- 1 egg
- ¼ cup light brown sugar
- ¼ cup granulated white sugar
- 2 tablespoons ground cinnamon
- ¼ teaspoon salt
- 3 cups bread flour
- 2 teaspoons bread machine yeast

Directions

Place all ingredients in the baking pan of the bread machine in the order recommended by the manufacturer.

Place the baking pan in the bread machine and close the lid.
Select Sweet Bread setting and then Medium Crust. Press the START button.

Carefully, remove the baking pan from the machine and then invert the bread loaf onto a wire rack to cool completely before slicing.

With a sharp knife, cut bread loaf into desired-sized slices and serve.

Calories: 195
Fat: 5 g
Protein: 4 g
Carb: 33 g

73 - Molasses Bread

Servings 12 slices

Difficulty ● ○ ○

Preparation Time 5 m

Cooking Time 4 h

Ingredients

1/3 cup milk

¼ cup water

3 tablespoons molasses

3 tablespoons butter, softened

2 cups bread flour

1¾ cups whole-wheat flour

2 tablespoons white sugar

1 teaspoon salt

2¼ teaspoons quick-rising yeast

Directions

Place all ingredients in the baking pan of the bread machine in the order recommended by the manufacturer.

Place the baking pan in the bread machine and close the lid.
Select light browning setting.

Press the START button.

Carefully, remove the baking pan from the machine and then invert the bread loaf onto a wire rack to cool completely before slicing.

With a sharp knife, cut bread loaf into desired-sized slices and serve.

Calories: 195
Fat: 3 g
Protein: 4 g
Carb: 37 g

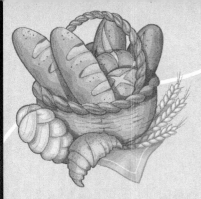

74 - Honey Bread

Servings 16 slices

Difficulty ● ○ ○

Preparation Time 5 m

Cooking Time 2 h

Ingredients

- 1 cup plus 1 tablespoon milk
- 3 tablespoons honey
- 3 tablespoons butter, melted
- 3 cups bread flour
- 1½ teaspoons salt
- 2 teaspoons active dry yeast

Directions

Place all ingredients in the baking pan of the bread machine in the order recommended by the manufacturer.

Place the baking pan in the bread machine and close the lid.

Select White Bread setting and then Medium Crust.
Press the START button.

Carefully, remove the baking pan from the machine and then invert the bread loaf onto a wire rack to cool completely before slicing.

With a sharp knife, cut bread loaf into desired-sized slices and serve.

Calories: 125
Fat: 3 g
Protein: 4 g
Carb: 27 g

75 - Maple Syrup Bread

Servings   12 slices

Difficulty   ● ● ○

Preparation Time   5 m

Cooking Time   3 h

Ingredients

- 1 cup buttermilk
- 2 tablespoons maple syrup
- 2 tablespoons vegetable oil
- 2 tablespoons non-fat dry milk powder
- 1 cup whole-wheat flour
- 2 cups bread flour
- 1 teaspoon salt
- 1½ teaspoons bread machine yeast

Directions

Place all ingredients in the baking pan of the bread machine in the order recommended by the manufacturer. Place the baking pan in the bread machine and close the lid.

Select Basic setting.
Press the START button.

Carefully, remove the baking pan from the machine and then invert the bread loaf onto a wire rack to cool completely before slicing.

With a sharp knife, cut bread loaf into desired-sized slices and serve.

Calories: 155
Fat: 3 g
Protein: 4 g
Carb: 27 g

76 - Raisin Bread

Servings 12 slices

Difficulty ● ● ○

Preparation Time 5 m

Cooking Time 3 h

Ingredients

- 1 cup water
- 2 tablespoons margarine
- 3 cups bread flour
- 3 tablespoons white sugar
- 1 teaspoon salt
- 1 teaspoon ground cinnamon
- 2½ teaspoons active dry yeast
- ¾ cup golden raisins

Directions

Place all ingredients (except for raisins) in the baking pan of the bread machine in the order recommended by the manufacturer.

Place the baking pan in the bread machine and close the lid.

Select Sweet Bread setting.
Press the START button.
Wait for the bread machine to beep before adding the raisins.

Carefully, remove the baking pan from the machine and then invert the bread loaf onto a wire rack to cool completely before slicing.

With a sharp knife, cut bread loaf into desired-sized slices and serve.

Calories: 175
Fat: 3 g
Protein: 4 g
Carb: 37 g

77 - Currant Bread

Servings 12 slices

Difficulty ● ● ○

Preparation Time 10 m

Cooking Time 3 h 30 m

Ingredients

1¼ cups warm milk

2 tablespoons light olive oil

2 tablespoons maple syrup

3 cups bread flour

2 teaspoons ground cardamom

1 teaspoon salt

2 teaspoons active dry yeast

½ cup currants

½ cup cashews, chopped finely

Directions

Place all ingredients (except for currants and cashews) in the baking pan of the bread machine in the order recommended by the manufacturer.

Place the baking pan in the bread machine and close the lid.

Select Basic setting.
Press the START button.
Wait for the bread machine to beep before adding the currants and cashews.

Carefully, remove the baking pan from the machine and then invert the bread loaf onto a wire rack to cool completely before slicing.

With a sharp knife, cut bread loaf into desired-sized slices and serve.

Calories: 232
Fat: 7 g
Protein: 6 g
Carb: 37 g

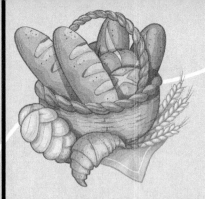

78 - Pineapple Juice Bread

Servings 12 slices

Difficulty ● ● ○

Preparation Time 10 m

Cooking Time 3 h 30 m

Ingredients

- 3/4 cup fresh pineapple juice
- 1 egg
- 2 tablespoons vegetable oil
- 2 1/2 tablespoons honey
- 3/4 teaspoon salt
- 3 cups bread flour
- 2 tablespoons dry milk powder
- 2 teaspoons quick-rising yeast

Directions

Place all ingredients in the baking pan of the bread machine in the order recommended by the manufacturer.

Place the baking pan in the bread machine and close the lid.

Select Sweet Bread setting and then Light Crust.

Press the START button.

Carefully, remove the baking pan from the machine and then invert the bread loaf onto a wire rack to cool completely before slicing.

With a sharp knife, cut bread loaf into desired-sized slices and serve.

Calories: 168
Fat: 2 g
Protein: 4 g
Carb: 30 g

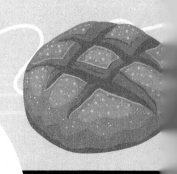

79 - Pumpkin Bread

Servings   14 slices

Difficulty ● ● ○

Preparation Time   15 m

Cooking Time 1 h

Ingredients

- ½ cup plus 2 tablespoons warm water
- ½ cup canned pumpkin puree
- ¼ cup butter, softened
- ¼ cup non-fat dry milk powder
- 2¾ cups bread flour
- ¼ cup brown sugar
- ¾ teaspoon salt
- 1 teaspoon ground cinnamon
- ½ teaspoon ground ginger
- 1/8 teaspoon ground nutmeg

2¼ teaspoons active dry yeast

Directions

Place all ingredients in the baking pan of the bread machine in the order recommended by the manufacturer.

Place the baking pan in the bread machine and close the lid.

Select Basic setting.
Press the START button.

Carefully, remove the baking pan from the machine and then invert the bread loaf onto a wire rack to cool completely before slicing.

With a sharp knife, cut bread loaf into desired-sized slices and serve.

Calories: 138
Fat: 2 g
Protein: 4 g
Carb: 22 g

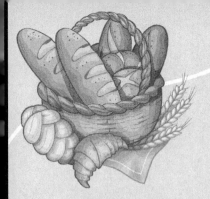

80 - Pumpkin Cranberry Bread

Servings   14 slices

Difficulty   ● ● ○

Preparation Time   15 m

Cooking Time   4 h

Ingredients

- ¾ cup water
- 2/3 cup canned pumpkin
- 3 tablespoons brown sugar
- 2 tablespoons vegetable oil
- 2 cups all-purpose flour
- 1 cup whole-wheat flour
- 1¼ teaspoon salt
- ½ cup sweetened dried cranberries
- ½ cup walnuts, chopped
- 1¾ teaspoons active dry yeast

Directions

Place all ingredients in the baking pan of the bread machine in the order recommended by the manufacturer.

Place the baking pan in the bread machine and close the lid.

Select Basic setting.
Press the START button.

Carefully, remove the baking pan from the machine and then invert the bread loaf onto a wire rack to cool completely before slicing.

With a sharp knife, cut bread loaf into desired-sized slices and serve.

Calories: 199
Fat: 2 g
Protein: 5 g
Carb: 31 g

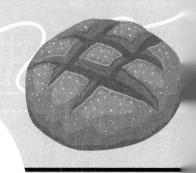

81 - Cranberry Bread

Servings   16 slices

Difficulty   ● ○ ○

Preparation Time   15 m

Cooking Time   3 h

Ingredients

1 cup plus 3 tablespoons water

¼ cup honey

2 tablespoons butter, softened

4 cups bread flour

1 teaspoon salt

2 teaspoons bread machine yeast

¾ cup dried cranberries

Directions

Place all ingredients (except the cranberries) in the baking pan of the bread machine in the order recommended by the manufacturer.

Place the baking pan in the bread machine and close the lid.

Select sweet bread setting.
Press the START button.

Wait for the bread machine to beep before adding the cranberries.

Carefully, remove the baking pan from the machine and then invert the bread loaf onto a wire rack to cool completely before slicing.

With a sharp knife, cut bread loaf into desired-sized slices and serve.

Calories: 147
Fat: 2 g
Protein: 4 g
Carb: 31 g

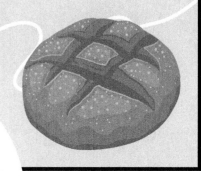

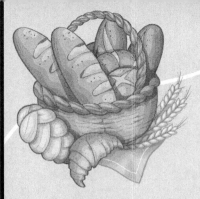

82 - Cranberry Orange Bread

Servings 12 slices

Difficulty ●○○

Preparation Time 15 m

Cooking Time 3 h

Ingredients

- 3 cups all-purpose flour
- 1 cup dried cranberries
- ¾ cup plain yogurt
- ½ cup warm water
- 3 tablespoons honey
- 1 tablespoon butter, melted
- 2 teaspoons active dry yeast
- 1½ teaspoons salt
- 1 teaspoon orange oil

Directions

Place all ingredients in the baking pan of the bread machine in the order recommended by the manufacturer.

Place the baking pan in the bread machine and close the lid.

Select Basic setting and then Light Crust. Press the START button.

Carefully, remove the baking pan from the machine and then invert the bread loaf onto a wire rack to cool completely before slicing.

With a sharp knife, cut bread loaf into desired-sized slices and serve.

Calories: 166
Fat: 2 g
Protein: 4 g
Carb: 31 g

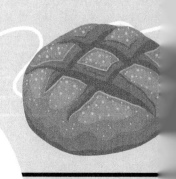

83 - Orange Bread

Servings 12 slices

Difficulty ● ● ○

Preparation Time 10 m

Cooking Time 3 h

Ingredients

- 1¼ cups water
- 3 tablespoons powdered milk
- 1½ tablespoons vegetable oil
- 3 tablespoons honey
- 2½ cups bread flour
- ¾ cup amaranth flour
- 1/3 cup whole-wheat flour
- ¾ teaspoon salt
- 3 tablespoons fresh orange zest, grated finely
- 2¼ teaspoons active dry yeast

Directions

Place all ingredients in the baking pan of the bread machine in the order recommended by the manufacturer.

Place the baking pan in the bread machine and close the lid.

Select Basic setting.
Press the START button.

Carefully, remove the baking pan from the machine and then invert the bread loaf onto a wire rack to cool completely before slicing.

With a sharp knife, cut bread loaf into desired-sized slices and serve.

Calories: 199
Fat: 2 g
Protein: 3 g
Carb: 40 g

84 - Banana Chocolate Chip Bread

Servings 16 slices

Difficulty ● ● ○

Preparation Time 10 m

Cooking Time 1 h 40 m

Ingredients

- ½ cup warm milk
- 2 eggs
- ½ cup butter, melted
- 1 teaspoon vanilla extract
- 3 medium ripe bananas, peeled and mashed
- 1 cup granulated white sugar
- 2 cups all-purpose flour
- ½ teaspoon salt
- 2 teaspoons baking powder
- 1 teaspoon baking soda
- ½ cup chocolate chips

Directions

Add ingredients (except for cranberries) in the baking pan of the bread machine in the order recommended by the manufacturer.

Place the baking pan in the bread machine and close the lid.

Select Quick Bread setting. Press the START button.

Wait for the bread machine to beep before adding the chocolate chips.

Carefully, remove the baking pan from the machine and then invert the bread loaf onto a wire rack to cool completely before slicing.

With a sharp knife, cut bread loaf into desired-sized slices and serve.

Calories: 215
Fat: 2 g
Protein: 3 g
Carb: 30 g

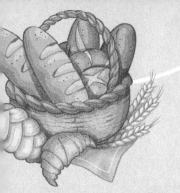

85 - Sweet Potato Bread

Servings 16 slices

Difficulty ● ● ○

Preparation Time 10 m

Cooking Time 3 h

Ingredients

- ½ cup warm water
- 1 teaspoon pure vanilla extract
- 1 cup boiled sweet potato, peeled, and mashed
- 4 cups bread flour
- ½ teaspoon ground cinnamon
- 2 tablespoons butter, softened
- 1/3 cup brown sugar
- 1 teaspoon salt
- 2 teaspoons active dry yeast
- 2 tablespoons powdered milk

Directions

Place all ingredients in the baking pan of the bread machine in the order recommended by the manufacturer.

Place the baking pan in the bread machine and close the lid.

Select White Bread setting.
Press the START button.

Carefully, remove the baking pan from the machine and then invert the bread loaf onto a wire rack to cool completely before slicing.

With a sharp knife, cut bread loaf into desired-sized slices and serve.

Calories: 150
Fat: 2 g
Protein: 3 g
Carb: 32 g

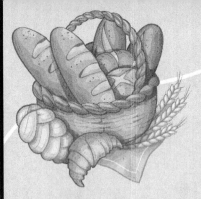

86 - Gingerbread

Servings 12 slices

Difficulty ● ○ ○

Preparation Time 10 m

Cooking Time 3 h

Ingredients

- 3/4 cup milk
- 1/4 cup molasses
- 1 egg
- 3 tablespoons butter
- 3 1/3 cups bread flour
- 1 tablespoon brown sugar
- ¾ teaspoon salt
- ¾ teaspoon ground cinnamon
- ¾ teaspoon ground ginger
- 2¼ teaspoons active dry yeast
- 1/3 cup raisins

Directions

Place all ingredients (except for raisins) in the baking pan of the bread machine in the order recommended by the manufacturer.

Place the baking pan in the bread machine and close the lid.

Select Basic setting and then Light Crust.
Press the START button.

Wait for the bread machine to beep before adding the raisins.

Carefully, remove the baking pan from the machine and then invert the bread loaf onto a wire rack to cool completely before slicing.

With a sharp knife, cut bread loaf into desired-sized slices and serve.

Calories: 150
Fat: 2 g
Protein: 3 g
Carb: 32 g

87 - Chocolate Chip Bread

Servings 12 slices

Difficulty ● ○ ○

Preparation Time 15 m

Cooking Time 2 h 50 m

Ingredients

- 1 cup milk
- ¼ cup water
- 1 egg, beaten
- 2 tablespoons butter, softened
- 3 cups bread flour
- 2 tablespoons white sugar
- 1 teaspoon salt
- 1 teaspoon ground cinnamon
- 1½ teaspoons active dry yeast
- ¾ cup semi-sweet mini chocolate chips

Directions

Put ingredients (except the chocolate chips) in the baking pan of the bread machine in the order recommended by the manufacturer.

Place the baking pan in the bread machine and close the lid.

Select Mix Bread setting.
Press the START button.

Wait for the bread machine to beep before adding chocolate chips.

Carefully, remove the baking pan from the machine and then invert the bread loaf onto a wire rack to cool completely before slicing.

With a sharp knife, cut bread loaf into desired-sized slices and serve.

Calories: 226
Fat: 2 g
Protein: 4 g
Carb: 36 g

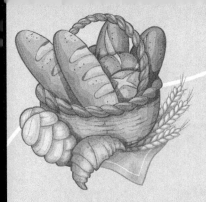

88 - Seed and Nut Bread

Servings   16 slices

Difficulty ● ○ ○

Preparation Time 15 m

Cooking Time 40 m

Ingredients

- 3 eggs
- 1 cup milk
- ¼ cup water
- 1 egg, beaten
- 2 tablespoons butter, softened
- 3 cups bread flour
- 2 tablespoons white sugar
- 1 teaspoon salt
- 1 teaspoon ground cinnamon
- 1½ teaspoons active dry yeast
- ¾ cup semi-sweet mini chocolate chips

Directions

Preheat the oven to 325F. Line a loaf pan with parchment paper.

In a giant bowl, whisk together the oil, eggs, psyllium husk powder, vinegar, salt, and liquid stevia.

Stir in the pepitas, almonds, sunflower seeds, and flaxseeds until well combined.

Dispense the batter into the prepared loaf pan, smooth it out and let it rest for 2 minutes.

Bake for 40 minutes.
Cool, slice, and serve.

Calories: 131
Fat: 6 g
Protein: 5 g
Carb: 28 g

89 - Pizza Basis

Servings 2

Difficulty ● ○ ○

Preparation Time 10 m

Cooking Time 1 h 20 m

Ingredients

- 1 ¼ cups warm water
- 2 cups flour
- 1 cup Semolina flour
- ½ teaspoon sugar
- 1 teaspoon salt
- 1 teaspoon olive oil
- 2 teaspoons yeast

Directions

Place all the ingredients in the bread maker's bucket in the order recommended by the manufacturer.

Select the Dough program.

After the dough has risen, use it as the base for the pizza.

Calories: 718
Fat: 6 g
Protein: 20 g
Carb: 141 g

90 - Italian Pie Calzone

Servings 12 slices

Difficulty ● ● ○

Preparation Time 10 m

Cooking Time 45 m

Ingredients

- 1 ¼ cups water
- 1 teaspoon salt
- 3 cups flour
- 1 teaspoon milk powder
- 1 ½ tablespoons sugar
- 2 teaspoons yeast
- ¾ cup tomato sauce for pizza
- 1 cup pepperoni sausage, finely chopped
- 1 ¼ cups grated mozzarella
- 2 tablespoons butter, melted

Directions

Put water, salt, bread baking flour, soluble milk, sugar, and yeast in the bread maker's bucket in the order recommended by the manufacturer.

Select the Dough setting.
After the end of the cycle, roll the dough on a lightly floured surface; form a rectangle measuring 45 x 25 cm.

Transfer to a lightly oiled baking tray. In a small bowl, combine the chopped pepperoni and mozzarella. Spoon the pizza sauce in a strip along the center of the dough. Add the filling of sausage and cheese.

Make diagonal incisions at a distance of 1 ½ cm from each other at the sides, receding 1 ½ cm from the filling.

Cross the strips on top of the filling, moistening it with the water. Lubricate with melted butter.

For 35 to 45 minutes bake at 360 degree F.

Calories: 247
Fat: 6 g
Protein: 7 g
Carb: 32 g

91 - French Baguettes

Servings 6 slices

Difficulty ● ● ○

Preparation Time 20 m

Cooking Time 2 h 30 m

Ingredients

- 1½ cups water
- 1½ teaspoons sugar
- 1½ teaspoons salt
- 3½ cups flour
- 1½ teaspoons yeast
- a mixture of different seeds (pumpkin, sunflower, black and white sesame)

Calories: 272
Fat: 2 g
Protein: 7 g
Carb: 57 g

Directions

To prepare the dough for French baguettes in the bread maker, place all the ingredients in the bread maker's container in order: water, salt, and sugar, flour, yeast. Select the Yeast Dough program. After 1½ hour, the dough for baguettes is ready.

Heat the oven to 440°F. Divide the dough into 2 parts. Lubricate the pan with oil. From the dough, form two French baguettes. Put on a baking pan and let it come for 10 minutes.

Then with a sharp knife, make shallow incisions on the surface of the baguettes. Sprinkle with water and sprinkle with a mixture of seeds. Leave it for another 10 minutes.

After the oven is warmed, put the pan with French baguettes in the oven for 5-7 minutes, then lower the heat to 360°F and bake for another 20-30 minutes until ready.

Transfer baguettes to a grate and cool. Your crispy, delicious, fragrant French baguettes are ready… Bon Appetit!

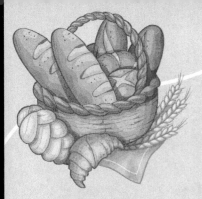

92 - Unleavened Cornbread

Servings 12 slices

Difficulty ● ○ ○

Preparation Time 10 m

Cooking Time 25 m

Ingredients

- 1 cup cornmeal
- 1 cup all-purpose flour
- 1/4 cup white sugar
- 1 teaspoon salt
- 1 egg
- 1/4 cup shortening, melted
- 1 cup milk

Directions

Preheat the oven at temperature 425 degrees F (220 degrees C). Lubricate a 12 cup muffin pan or line with muffin papers.

Using a large bowl, stir together the cornmeal, flour, sugar and salt. Make a well in the mid and pour in the egg, shortening and milk.

Stir until well blended. Spoon batter into the prepared muffin cups.

Bake for 20 to 25 minutes until a toothpick inserted into the middle of a muffin comes out clean.

Calories: 150
Fat: 2 g
Protein: 5 g
Carb: 22 g

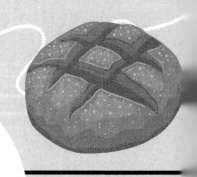

93 - Vegan Corn Bread

Servings 4 slices

Difficulty ● ○ ○

Preparation Time 10 m

Cooking Time 15 m

Ingredients

- Cooking spray
- 1 egg
- 1 tablespoon coconut flour
- 1 tablespoon almond flour
- 1 tablespoon almond milk
- 1 tablespoon butter, melted
- ¼ teaspoon baking powder
- A pinch of salt
- 1 tablespoon broccoli, chopped
- 1 tablespoon mozzarella, grated

Directions

By means of a bowl, mix the almond flour with the coconut flour, baking powder, salt, broccoli and the mozzarella and stir.

Put the remaining ingredients except the cooking spray and stir everything really well.

Grease a loaf pan with cooking spray, pour the bread batter, cook at 400 F degrees f for 15 minutes, cool down and serve.

Calories: 244
Fat: 2 g
Protein: 6 g
Carb: 22 g

94 - Milk and Honey Bread

Servings 1 loaf

Difficulty ● ○ ○

Preparation Time 10 m

Cooking Time 3 h 20 m

Ingredients

- 3 ½ cups whole wheat flour
- 3 tablespoons sugar
- 1 ½ teaspoons salt
- 1 cup plus 1 tablespoo milk
- ½ cup (half and half
- 3 tablespoons (42 grams) softened butter, salted or unsalted
- 1 ½ teaspoons instant yeast or active dry

Directions

By means of a bowl, mix the almond flour with the coconut flour, baking powder, salt, broccoli and the mozzarella and stir.

Put the remaining ingredients except the cooking spray and stir everything really well.

Grease a loaf pan with cooking spray, pour the bread batter, cook at 400 F degrees f for 15 minutes, cool down and serve.

Calories: 244
Fat: 2 g
Protein: 6 g
Carb: 22 g

95 - Banana Bread

Servings 10 slices

Difficulty ● ○ ○

Preparation Time 10 m

Cooking Time 50 m

Ingredients

- ½ cup + 2 tbsp butter, softened, plus extra for the tin
- ½ cup + 3 tbsp caster sugar
- 2 large eggs, beaten
- ¾ cup + 2 tbsp self-raising flour
- 1 tsp baking powder
- 2 very ripe bananas, mashed
- ¼ cup icing sugar
- handful dried banana chips, for decoration

Directions

Butter a 2lb loaf tin and line the base and sides with baking parchment.

Cream softened butter and caster sugar until fluffy, then slowly add 2 large eggs with a little of the flour. Fold in the remaining flour, 1 tsp baking powder and 2 mashed bananas.

Pour the mixture into the prepared tin and bake for about 45-50 mins. Check the loaf at 5-min intervals from around 30-40 mins in the oven by testing it with a skewer.

Cool in the tin for 15 mins, then remove to a wire rack.

Mix ¼ cup + 1 tbsp sugar with 3 tsp water to make a runny icing.

Drizzle the icing across the top of the cake and decorate with a handful of banana chips.

Calories: 269
Fat: 13
Protein: 3 g
Carb: 34 g

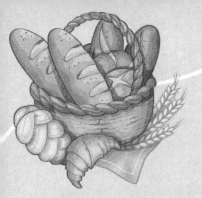

96 - Salt Crusted Bread

Servings 12 slices

Difficulty ● ○ ○

Preparation Time 10 m

Cooking Time 3 h

Ingredients

- 1 1/3 Cups - Water
- 3 Cups - Flour
- 4 Tablespoons Butter (sliced)
- 1 Teaspoon Salt
- 1 Cup Oatmeal
- 1/3 Cup Sugar
- 1 1/2 Teaspoons Yeast
- 1/4 Teaspoon - Coarse Food-Grade Salt

Directions

- Add all ingredients starting with the water into the bread machine.
- Press the START button after entering the correct settings

After the bread machine has finished baking the bread, remove the bread and place it on a cooling rack.

Calories: 189
Fat: 2
Protein: 5 g
Carb: 28 g

97 - Extra Buttery White Bread

Servings 16 slices

Difficulty ● ○ ○

Preparation Time 15 m

Cooking Time 3 h

Ingredients

- 1 1/8 cups milk
- 4 Tablespoon unsalted butter
- 3 cups bread flour
- 1½ Tablespoon white granulated sugar
- 1½ teaspoon salt
- 1½ teaspoon bread machine yeast

Directions

Soften the butter in your microwave.

Add each ingredient to the bread machine in the order and at the temperature recommended by your bread machine manufacturer.

Close the lid, select the basic or white bread, medium crust setting on your bread machine, and press START.

When the bread machine has finished baking, remove the bread and put it on a cooling rack.

Calories: 104
Fat: 1 g
Protein: 4 g
Carb: 22 g

CONCLUSION

Depending on what kind of home baker you are, bread is either a must-know rite of passage, or an intimidating goal you haven't quite worked up the courage to try. This is because bread is a labor-intensive food where slight mistakes can have a big impact on the final result. Most of us rely on store-bought bread, but once you've tasted homemade bread, it's tempting to make your own as often as possible. A bread machine makes the process easier.

Making a loaf of bread feels like a major accomplishment. Why? There are a lot of steps. Mixing, kneading, proofing, resting, shaping, and finally baking.

You know how to make bread by hand, so how does the bread-making machine do it? A bread machine is basically a small, electric oven. It fits one large bread tin with a special axle connected to the electric motor. A metal paddle connects to the axle, and this is what kneads the dough. If you were making the bread in a mixer, you would probably use a dough hook, and in some instructions, you'll see the bread machine's kneading part referred as a hook or "blades."

The first thing you do is take out the tin and add the bread dough you made in Step 1. Bread machines can make any kind of bread, whether it's made from normal white flour, whole wheat, etc. Pop this tin unto the axle and program by selecting the type of bread, which includes options like basic, whole-wheat, multigrain, and so on. There are even cycles specifically for sweet breads; breads with nuts, seeds, and raisins; gluten-free; and bagels. Many models also let you cook jam.

You'll probably see a "dough" mode option, too. You would use that one for pizza. The machine doesn't actually cook anything; it just kneads and then you take out the pizza dough and bake it in your normal oven. If you aren't making pizza dough, the next selections you'll make are the loaf size and crust type. Once those are chosen, press the "timer" button. Based on your other selections, a time will show up and all you have to do is push "START."

After kneading and before the machine begins baking, many people will remove the dough so they can take out the kneading paddles, since they often make an indent in the finished bread. The paddles should simply pop out or you can buy a special hook that makes the removal easier. Now you can return the bread to the machine. The lid is closed during the baking process. If it's a glass lid, you can actually see what's going on. You'll hear the paddle spinning on the motor, kneading the dough. It lies still for the rising stage, and then starts again for more kneading if necessary.

The motor is also off for the proving stage. Next, the heating element switches on, and steam rises from the exhaust vent as the bread bakes. The whole process usually takes a few hours.

There's a lot of work involved in making bread by hand. When you use a machine, that machine does a lot of the busy stuff for you. You just add your dough and the bread maker starts doing its thing, giving you time to do other chores or sit back and relax. As a note, not all bread makers are completely automatic, so if you want this benefit, you'll probably have to pay a bit more money. It's worth it for a lot of people, though.

THANK YOU FOR READING THIS BOOK
AND I HOPE YOU ENJOYED IT.

I WOULD BE VERY GRATEFUL IF YOU COULD
LEAVE ME A REVIEW ON AMAZON.
THANK YOU!!!

CONVERSION TABLES

QUANTITY

1 cup = 16 tablespoon

1 cup = 48 teaspoon

1/2 cup = 8 tablespoon

1/2 cup = 24 teaspoon

1/4 cup =4 tablespoon

1/4 cup = 12 teaspoon

1/8 cup = 2 tablespoon

1/8 cup = 6 teaspoon

1 tablespoon = 3 teaspoon

1/2 tablespoon = 1-1/2 teaspoon

WEIGHT

1 oz =28 g

5 oz= 141 g

10 oz = 283 g

11 oz = 312 g

12 oz = 340 g =3/4 Lb

13 oz = 369 g

14 oz = 397 g

15 oz = 425 g

24 oz = 680 g =1-1/2 Lb

26 oz = 750 g

32 oz = 907 g =2 Lb

35 oz = 1000 g

TEMPERATURE

212° F =100° C

230° F =110° C

248° F =120° C

266° F =130° C

284° F =140° C

302° F =150° C

320° F =160° C

338° F =170° C

356° F = 180° C

374° F =190° C

392° F =200° C

410° F =210° C

428° F =220° C

446° F =230° C

Printed in Great Britain
by Amazon

22718915R00077